A Kingdom Bestowed

A KINGDOM BESTOWED

David Meets Abigail

Mark Belz

FOREWORD BY
Jackie Robertson

RESOURCE *Publications* • Eugene, Oregon

A KINGDOM BESTOWED
David Meets Abigail

Resource Publications
An Imprint of Wipf and Stock Publishers
199 W. 8th Ave., Suite 3
Eugene, OR 97401

www.wipfandstock.com

PAPERBACK ISBN: 978-1-6667-7850-2
HARDCOVER ISBN: 978-1-6667-7851-9
EBOOK ISBN: 978-1-6667-7852-6

06/05/23

All quoted scripture is from the English Standard Version, ©2001 by Crossway, a publishing ministry of Good News Publishers, Chicago IL, unless otherwise indicated.

CONTENTS

FOREWORD

MY HUSBAND GEORGE AND I were like deer in the headlights before an on-coming Mack truck called "parenthood." Two twenty somethings manag-ing demanding careers in occupational therapy and pastoral ministry and now responsible for a newborn who came fully assembled, but at least in our case, without an instruction booklet.

Among the many other grown-up things we had to think of now—life insurance, education savings, school districts—we had to prepare a will. So, there we were in our friend Mark's impressive conference room at his Clayton law office. Step by step, he walked us through the will he had drafted for us *pro bono* naming our son Taylor as the beneficiary. Of what, I'm not sure, but at least Mark assured us he would not be a ward of the state if we both kicked the bucket. When the last document was signed, Mark turned his chair to look at Taylor sleeping in his pumpkin seat (a rare event for the baby) and offered this soliloquy, "Look at him there. He has no idea we have taken care of all these legal arrangements to ensure his well-being. Isn't that just like the Father's care for us? We can't fathom how vulnerable we are in this world, but the Lord in his grace provides for our every need before we even ask." Though George had known Mark and his family for years before then, this was my first time to sit as his feet as a teacher . . . and I was hooked!

Some years later, Mark and his dear wife Linda would join our church. They had been involved in helping several churches get started and needed a place of respite. However, Mark couldn't sit and soak for long. In a couple of years, he was teaching Sunday School and helping George on the session. I took every class he offered—Romans, Job, Galatians, and a few other topical offerings. Mark's worldview shaped by our common alma mater Covenant College, his theology deepened by a degree from Covenant Theological Seminary where my husband obtained his degree too, his insights from practicing law, and practical wisdom gained from godly parents and good churches combined to make him a master teacher and applier of God's word. He wrings out a passage like I twist a lime into guacamole, trying to get every last drop. Few topics of biblical theology are left unexplored, and each lesson finds its way to the capstone of every verse of Scripture, the grace of God in Jesus Christ.

This book about Abigail is classic Mark Belz teaching. Without sappy allegory, Mark explores an array of biblical themes either explicit or alluded to in this fascinating narrative about the household of Nabal's near miss with genocide by the hand of David. Bible study, prayer, godly counsel, parenting, bullying, anger, addiction, use of the tongue, the Holy Spirit, prophecy, God's sovereignty, roles, and the certainty of Jesus' coming kingdom are just a selection of key subjects Mark guides the reader (and potentially a family in devotions) to apply biblically.

I'm not sure why our friend Mark would ask me to write this foreword. My husband says I reminded him of another woman in the Bible married to a fool! I don't think that's true. George is a wise man. At the same time, I know, like George, Mark is only as effective as he is because of the woman he's married to! I would rather think he asked me to write this because I am the mother of three adult daughters (one named Abigail!) who emulate the positive traits the book highlights about David's future wife. As any honest parent must admit, we cannot take much credit for whatever good results occur with our children. However, I would echo what Mark testifies to in this great book. Children who know they are loved unconditionally by their family, who are led to read his word and depend on the Spirit in prayer, who are surrounded by gracious believers in the church, and then imitate what they have experienced tend to flourish. It doesn't mean they will never stray, maybe even for a long time, but on the whole life goes better for them because it's the Lord's way.

And specifically, for women, I would say Mark exposes an encouraging and appropriately empowering role model in Abigail. When a woman is following the Holy Spirit's lead, she can stand up to any challenge. By biblical wisdom, she can also lead and instruct anyone in a faithful, even soul-saving direction. Our young women need this teaching so they can be change agents for Christ in the workplace, as single professionals, as moms, or with their husbands. Abigail's life is a foretaste of Pentecost when the Spirit's power poured out on the Church would embolden daughters to prophesy biblical truth with their lives and words.

Thank you, Mark, for this gift to your Church reminding us that our good Father has provided all our needs in Jesus before we have even asked—like the Spirit-created example of Abigail.

—Jackie Robertson

Memphis
Spring, 2023

PREFACE

BEFORE I BEGAN WRITING this book, I scoured the internet to see what had been written about the main character, Abigail. What I found surprised me. There were a few books that were devotional in nature, some "historical novels," and other writings setting Abigail as an example of what a believing woman should look like. Most of these were good and helpful. But they were not exegetical, nor did they claim to be. That fact encouraged me to proceed with the book, because I think a thorough exegesis of Abigail's story, found in First Samuel 25, is needed, and the most helpful and productive way to grasp who she was and what she had to say.

As I studied the passage and began to write, I soon saw that who this Jewish woman was and what she said was astonishing. She came on the scene in the Bible immediately after Israel's prophet and last judge, Samuel, had died. His death, in fact, is recorded in the first verse of Chapter 25, and marks a major transition in Israel's history. With Samuel's death, David was left without a mentor. The balance of Chapter 25 (41 verses) is devoted to the story of David's meeting with his future wife, Abigail. For a brief but crucial moment, she mentored Israel's future king. In a sense, she picked up where Samuel left off. He had to leave the game, and she made her first appearance in the Majors as his pinch-hitter.

What Abigail spoke to David was crucial to his life personally, and particularly to his future royal leadership of God's chosen people Israel. But she also speaks to us, three thousand years later. She has a worldview that is godly and eternal. Contrasted with an earthly worldview, it relieves believers from having to depend on themselves, and directs them to lean wholly upon God's everlasting wisdom, his immutable promises, and steadfast love. Her counsel in this passage proves to be a blueprint for David's "everlasting kingdom," that is, the church universal.

As we shall see, Abigail was a humble woman. She humbled herself before God as well as the future King David, and delivered a humble and eloquent plea as she was directed by the Holy Spirit. Because God had humbled David's heart, his ears were open to hear, understand, and happily yield to her plea. God had prepared both of them, and he himself is front and center in this tiny slice of Jewish history.

David had been anointed by the prophet Samuel prior to the Abigail story, but immediately after Samuel's death, he was about to make a left turn when he should have turned right. Her counsel corrected his course, thus delivering him from disaster. He had made a catastrophic decision without asking the Lord for guidance, but Abigail intervened with the guidance she had received from the Holy Spirit before David could carry it out.

Abigail's central message was that David's kingdom would not be merely David's kingdom, but God's. God would use David, but Abigail told David that God would do it all. David need not—and must not—take matters into his own hands. The Lord's kingdom would be "bestowed" upon David; he would not earn or build it himself. Thus it was that David's kingdom could be an everlasting gift, or, as Abigail put it, a "sure house." What Abigail said was what Jesus later said: "*I will build my church.*"

As I pondered Abigail's message to David delivered in about 1000 B.C., I was constantly impressed with just how timely and relevant her counsel is to us in the present era. As you read this book, think of the myriad ways in which we try to build our lives, our families, and the church, without inquiring of the Lord. Too often we attempt to do what is right in our own eyes, operating from an earthly worldview. I profited greatly from the advice Abigail gave David, and I trust that you will as well. And I trust that you, like David, will have open ears, eager to hear what God has to say.

†

I HAVE ALWAYS NEEDED help in my writing projects, because the art doesn't come easily for me. In this effort I have received invaluable counsel from Linda, my wife—the most talented writer I know. Her edits have helped to make the crooked straight, and the rough places plain. There was also my late kid brother Nat Belz, who went to heaven in March 2023 after a short but intense battle with cancer. Even when he was sick and in pain, he did what he could to get the book ready for publication. He obviously had more important things to do and think about, but he stuck with it as best he could. Nat was a helper not only to me throughout my life, but to many others as well, and he is already missed greatly.

Dr. Dan Doriani, professor at Covenant Theological Seminary, professed enthusiasm for the book (perhaps this was in part because the Dorianis have a daughter named Abigail). Whatever his reasons, Dan strongly urged me to continue with the book and get it published. Dr. Will Barker, former professor at and president of Covenant Seminary also assisted with edits, suggestion sand encouragement. If you discover any theological errors in the book, the author will have to refer you to these two studied theologians! Bob Korljan, a close friend and classmate of mine at Covenant Seminary in the late 1970's, is an ordained teaching elder in the Presbyterian Church of America. Bob gave valuable edits which has made the writing more precise than it otherwise would have been. And George Robertson, senior pastor of Second Presbyterian Church in Memphis, has read the manuscript and has been most helpful.

To all these precious friends, helpers and encouragers, I give my humble and grateful thanks.

ABIGAIL AND DAVID

The Text

THIS BOOK IS A STUDY of First Samuel 25, which contains the story of Abigail's encounter with David, prior to his becoming the king of Israel. Throughout the book, all quotations of scripture are from First Samuel 25 unless otherwise indicated. For the reader's convenience, the text is set out here in full.

FIRST SAMUEL 25

¹ Now Samuel died. And all Israel assembled and mourned for him, and they buried him in his house at Ramah. Then David rose and went down to the wilderness of Paran.

² And there was a man in Maon whose business was in Carmel. The man was very rich; he had three thousand sheep and a thousand goats. He was shearing his sheep in Carmel. ³ Now the name of the man was Nabal, and the name of his wife Abigail. The woman was discerning and beautiful, but the man was harsh and badly behaved; he was a Calebite. ⁴ David heard in the wilderness that Nabal was shearing his sheep. ⁵ So David sent ten young men. And David said to the young men, "Go up to Carmel, and go to Nabal and greet him in my name. ⁶ And thus you shall greet him: 'Peace be to you, and peace be to your house, and peace be to all that you have. ⁷ I hear that you have shearers. Now your shepherds have been with us, and we did them no harm, and they missed nothing all the time they were in Carmel. ⁸ Ask your young men, and they will tell you. Therefore let my young men

1

find favor in your eyes, for we come on a feast day. Please give whatever you have at hand to your servants and to your son David."'

⁹ When David's young men came, they said all this to Nabal in the name of David, and then they waited. ¹⁰ And Nabal answered David's servants, "Who is David? Who is the son of Jesse? There are many servants these days who are breaking away from their masters. ¹¹ Shall I take my bread and my water and my meat that I have killed for my shearers and give it to men who come from I do not know where?" ¹² So David's young men turned away and came back and told him all this. ¹³ And David said to his men, "Every man strap on his sword!" And every man of them strapped on his sword. David also strapped on his sword. And about four hundred men went up after David, while two hundred remained with the baggage.

¹⁴ But one of the young men told Abigail, Nabal's wife, "Behold, David sent messengers out of the wilderness to greet our master, and he railed at them. ¹⁵ Yet the men were very good to us, and we suffered no harm, and we did not miss anything when we were in the fields, as long as we went with them. ¹⁶ They were a wall to us both by night and by day, all the while we were with them keeping the sheep. ¹⁷ Now therefore know this and consider what you should do, for harm is determined against our master and against all his house, and he is such a worthless man that one cannot speak to him."

¹⁸ Then Abigail made haste and took two hundred loaves and two skins of wine and five sheep already prepared and five seahs of parched grain and a hundred clusters of raisins and two hundred cakes of figs, and laid them on donkeys. ¹⁹ And she said to her young men, "Go on before me; behold, I come after you." But she did not tell her husband Nabal.²⁰ And as she rode on the donkey and came down under cover of the mountain, behold, David and his men came down toward her, and she met them. ²¹ Now David had said, "Surely in vain have I guarded all that this fellow has in the wilderness, so that nothing was missed of all that belonged to him, and he has returned me evil for good. ²² God do so to the enemies of David and more also, if by morning I leave so much as one male of all who belong to him."

²³ When Abigail saw David, she hurried and got down from the donkey and fell before David on her face and bowed to the ground. ²⁴ She fell at his feet and said, "On me alone, my lord, be the guilt. Please let your servant speak in your ears, and hear the words of your servant. ²⁵ Let not my lord regard this worthless fellow, Nabal, for as his name is, so is he. Nabal is his

name, and folly is with him. But I your servant did not see the young men of my lord, whom you sent. ²⁶ Now then, my lord, as the LORD lives, and as your soul lives, because the LORD has restrained you from bloodguilt and from saving with your own hand, now then let your enemies and those who seek to do evil to my lord be as Nabal. ²⁷ And now let this present that your servant has brought to my lord be given to the young men who follow my lord. ²⁸ Please forgive the trespass of your servant. For the LORD will certainly make my lord a sure house, because my lord is fighting the battles of the LORD, and evil shall not be found in you so long as you live. ²⁹ If men rise up to pursue you and to seek your life, the life of my lord shall be bound in the bundle of the living in the care of the LORD your God. And the lives of your enemies he shall sling out as from the hollow of a sling. ³⁰ And when the LORD has done to my lord according to all the good that he has spoken concerning you and has appointed you prince over Israel, ³¹ my lord shall have no cause of grief or pangs of conscience for having shed blood without cause or for my lord working salvation himself. And when the LORD has dealt well with my lord, then remember your servant."

³² And David said to Abigail, "Blessed be the LORD, the God of Israel, who sent you this day to meet me! ³³ Blessed be your discretion, and blessed be you, who have kept me this day from bloodguilt and from working salvation with my own hand! ³⁴ For as surely as the LORD, the God of Israel, lives, who has restrained me from hurting you, unless you had hurried and come to meet me, truly by morning there had not been left to Nabal so much as one male." ³⁵ Then David received from her hand what she had brought him. And he said to her, "Go up in peace to your house. See, I have obeyed your voice, and I have granted your petition."

³⁶ And Abigail came to Nabal, and behold, he was holding a feast in his house, like the feast of a king. And Nabal's heart was merry within him, for he was very drunk. So she told him nothing at all until the morning light. ³⁷ In the morning, when the wine had gone out of Nabal, his wife told him these things, and his heart died within him, and he became as a stone. ³⁸ And about ten days later the LORD struck Nabal, and he died.

³⁹ When David heard that Nabal was dead, he said, "Blessed be the LORD who has avenged the insult I received at the hand of Nabal, and has kept back his servant from wrongdoing. The LORD has returned the evil of Nabal on his own head." Then David sent and spoke to Abigail, to take her as his

wife. [40] When the servants of David came to Abigail at Carmel, they said to her, "David has sent us to you to take you to him as his wife." [41] And she rose and bowed with her face to the ground and said, "Behold, your handmaid is a servant to wash the feet of the servants of my lord." [42] And Abigail hurried and rose and mounted a donkey, and her five young women attended her. She followed the messengers of David and became his wife.

PROLOGUE

Farewell to a Judge

"NOW SAMUEL DIED," the text begins, so that is where we will begin. Some think that verse one of Chapter twenty-five should be included at the end of Chapter twenty-four, but I think that the author's mention of Samuel's death is appropriately placed at the beginning of the story we will study, David's meeting with Abigail.

Judges had led and ruled Israel from the time of Joshua on, up until Saul became king, a period of about four hundred years. Their "appointment" to the office is a mystery; the Bible doesn't mention how they were selected, although God was the one who appointed them.[1] There is no record in scripture of their anointment or any other formal indicia of office. Nevertheless, they served both as rulers and priests. They were not legislators; the law had already been established by Moses, who had received it by direct revelation from God.

The book of Judges mentions twelve of these judges,[2] but there were others. First Samuel identifies four more: Eli, Samuel and Samuel's sons, Joel and Abijah. First Chronicles mentions Kenaniah and his sons (no number is given), and Second Chronicles includes two more: Amariah and Zebadiah.

Samuel, Israel's last recorded judge,[3] had judged Israel for more than forty years when he died. Very likely, that was longer than any of the other

---

1. 2 Sam 7:11.

2. Othniel, Ehud, Shamgar, Deborah, Gideon, Tola, Jair, Jephthah, Ibzan, Elon, Abdon, and Samson. Gideon's illegitimate son Abimilech also served as a judge after Gideon's death.

3. Additionally, Samuel was acknowledged as a prophet: "And all Israel from Dan to

5

judges' reigns. His death marked the end not only of the period of the judges, but the end of Israel's history as a theocracy.[4] From Egypt on God himself was King of the realm. Both Samuel and the Lord lamented the end of Israel's being ruled directly from on high, and we might expect that every citizen in the land would lament it as well, but not so. The populace preferred that God not interfere so directly in their lives. They demanded an earthly king. They wanted to be like all the nations around them, and God, while warning them of the consequences, gave them what they wanted.

Sadly, part of the blame for Israel's demand for a king rested on Samuel himself, even though God would graciously deliver him from taking responsibility.[5] His two sons had become judges, as mentioned above, but they had not been trained "in the way [they] should go,"[6] for when they were old they *did* depart from the way they should go by perverting justice for personal gain.[7] The citizenry had accepted Samuel's righteous reign, but could not bear up under his sons Joel and Abijah.[8] Then, because of the sins of Samuel's sons, the people of Israel amplified their sin by demanding a king. Sin begets sin.

But God is sovereign, and he often redeems sin for his children's ultimate good.[9] He was doing so when he told Samuel to give them what they

---

Beersheba knew that Samuel was established as a prophet of the Lord" (1 Sam 3:20). He also regularly performed the priestly function. In 1 Sam 13:14-15 he rebuked Saul for not waiting for him (Samuel) to offer a sacrifice before battle.

4. There are varying definitions of the term "theocracy," but it is used here to refer to God's direct rule over his people, not, for example, a kingdom or nation only under his law.

5. "[The people] have not rejected you, but they have rejected me from being king over them" (1 Kgs 8:7b).

6. "Train up a child in the way he should go; even when he is old he will not depart from it" (Prov 22:6).

7. "When Samuel became old, he made his sons judges over Israel. The name of his firstborn son was Joel, and the name of his second, Abijah; they were judges in Beersheba. Yet his sons did not walk in his ways but turned aside after gain. They took bribes and perverted justice" (1 Sam 8:1-3).

8. Scripture specifies this as the moving reason for the people's demand for a king. They told Samuel, "Behold, you are old and your sons do not walk in your ways. Now appoint for us a king to judge us like all the nations" (1 Kgs 8:5b).

9. The prime example of this is the crucifixion of Jesus, which God used not only to fulfill Old Testament prophecy but to bring salvation to the world. The Apostle Paul said: "Brothers, sons of the family of Abraham, and those among you who fear God, to us has been sent the message of this salvation. For those who live in Jerusalem and their rulers, because they did not recognize him *nor understand the utterances of the prophets*, which

demanded.[10] Though Samuel wasn't aware of it at the time, God was establishing the Davidic kingdom, which, through Christ, would be eternal.[11]

Though Samuel lamented the people's demand, he obeyed God's command and set about the business of finding a suitable ruler.[12] Establishing the kingship meant the end of God's direct rule over Israel. We could say that Samuel was called upon to preside over the death of the theocracy. But I think that what appeared to be an ending was really an "official time out," the kind we see in a football game. The play-by-play person always says, "Stay tuned. We'll be right back!" (and then the insufferably long break for commercials).

From Adam through Samuel, God ruled directly over his people. When he spoke to humankind it was direct, and his rule was direct. For example, he spoke "one-on-one" to Adam, Eve, Cain, Noah, Abraham, Isaac, Jacob, and ruled over them directly. There appears to have been a shift when Moses entered the picture, 400 years after Jacob. Moses received the words of God and for the last forty years of his life faithfully transmitted the words of Yahweh to the Israelites just as God had spoken them to him. Of course, he also ruled over God's chosen race, but with little wiggle room.

---

are read every Sabbath, *fulfilled them by condemning him.* And though they found in him no guilt worthy of death, they asked Pilate to have him executed. And *when they had carried out all that was written of him,* they took him down from the tree and laid him in a tomb" (Acts 13:26-29) (emphases added).

10. 1 Sam 8:9.

11. Through the prophet Nathan, God told David: "When your days are fulfilled and you lie down with your fathers, I will raise up your offspring after you, who shall come from your body, and I will establish his kingdom. He shall build a house for my name, and I will establish the throne of his kingdom forever" (2 Sam 7:12-16). *See also* 2 Chr 13:5, Ps 89:20-37, 1 Kgs 9:4-7, 1 Chr 28:5 and 2 Chr 7:17.

12. God knew that the Israelites would demand a king, and sanctioned it 400 years before they did so: "When you come to the land that the LORD your God is giving you, and you possess it and dwell in it and then say, 'I will set a king over me, like all the nations that are around me,' you may indeed set a king over you whom the LORD your God will choose. One from among your brothers you shall set as king over you. You may not put a foreigner over you, who is not your brother. Only he must not acquire many horses for himself or cause the people to return to Egypt in order to acquire many horses, since the LORD has said to you, 'You shall never return that way again.' And he shall not acquire many wives for himself, lest his heart turn away, nor shall he acquire for himself excessive silver and gold" (Deut 14:14-17). This passage is not just directive, but prophetic. Solomon, Israel's third king, acquired many wives and excessive silver and gold.

Yahweh told him exactly what to say and do. God remained the king, ruling through a servant that "was faithful in all God's house."[13]

Thus it is that we can say that the first verse of the text, First Samuel 25:1, records an epochal turning point in eschatology. God's direct kingly rule over his people ended as the Kingdom of Israel was initiated, for God told Samuel "they *have rejected me from being king* over them."[14] This appears to mean two things: (a) God had ruled directly as king over Israel up through Samuel, and (b) God's direct rule as king over Israel was ending because the people rejected him. And though sin brought it about, this change was in God's sovereign plan. Of course, God did not—nor will he ever—relinquish the throne. He is the eternal Sovereign over all. But he can change the immediate manner of administration of his kingdom. Jesus said, "I will build my church,"[15] but throughout the Old and New Testaments, up to present, he has used human agencies to execute his rule.

This turning point is set forth poetically in the text: "*And Samuel died . . . And David rose*" (v.1). But while "and Samuel died" meant the end of God's direct rule, we also know that it was the "end" only until the Second Coming. God's direct rule not only over his own but all the earth will make a new and glorious entry upon Christ's return, when "The kingdom of the world has become the kingdom of our Lord and of his Christ, and he shall reign forever and ever."[16] Handel, in composing *Messiah*, thought that was worth multiple "Hallelujahs"!

But as in the football game mentioned above, this seems to be a *long* time out. So far it has been more than three thousand years since the death of Samuel (though from God's perspective perhaps it has been only three days).[17] To us this is an excruciatingly long wait, and we earthlings are not alone because even those souls already in heaven cry out "Lord, how long?"[18]

With Samuel's death, David had no mentor, no one like Samuel to give him advice, no one like him to guide him in the decisions he would be

---

13. Heb 3:2b.

14. 1 Sam 8:7b (emphasis added).

15. Matt 16:18.

16. Rev 11:15b.

17. "But do not overlook this one fact, beloved, that with the Lord one day is as a thousand years, and a thousand years as one day" (2 Pet 3:8).

18. "[T]he souls in heaven cried out with a loud voice, 'O Sovereign Lord, holy and true, how long before you will judge and avenge our blood on those who dwell on the earth?'" (Rev 6: 10).

required to make. He had himself to rely on, of course, but he was young and inexperienced. He surely knew that God was with him, but when he was of a sudden deprived of the man who served as his spiritual father and mentor, he was susceptible to error. In part, I believe, that is what we see happening in this story. David was vulnerable. He believed he had to forge ahead on his own, and in so doing made a bad decision. There was no one around who could check his judgment, or steer him in the right direction.

It is telling that after Samuel's funeral "David rose and went down to the wilderness of Paran" (v.1). Physically, he was literally in the wilderness. But he was also in the wilderness mentally and spiritually. He was alone out there, even though he had a band of 600 men, and was being hounded by Saul who was determined to do him in. He was badly in need of a godly advisor or two, to help steer him in the right direction. With Samuel in the grave, he believed he had no one to help. He felt he had to look to himself for guidance.

But there actually was One around who could help. Though you couldn't see him or hear him speak audibly, he was right there with David. He had spoken directly to David previously, and would do so in the future, but this time he chose to speak through his servant Abigail. We will see how God told her to meet up with David to help him avoid an error he was about to make, to show him how to get back on track. And God himself would give Abigail the words to say.

Thus the story of Abigail is most significant. She appears in Scripture right at the time of this turning point, that is, the end of God's direct rule over his chosen people and the initiation of the Davidic kingdom. Her message, as given to her by the Holy Spirit, represents the first prophetic word given to God's people at the beginning of a new era. God used her to set David straight when he veered off course. But her message also helped to set David's coming kingdom, then Israel as a nation, and then the church, in the right direction on some crucial matters.

As we shall see, her caution to David stands as a caution to us: we cannot depend on ourselves, we cannot build our own kingdom, and we cannot substitute our own judgment for God's. As David would learn through his meeting with Abigail, "[t]here is a way that seems right to a man, but its end is the way to death."[19]

19. Prov 14:12.

1. DAVID'S EDUCATION

Wen David became the king of Israel at age thirty in 1010 B.C., he didn't parachute in from nowhere and suddenly appear as commander in chief. He had been somewhere. He had traveled a long and sometimes painful road.

In God's sovereign plan, even before he was born, David was set to become King of Israel. That was determined from eternity past. But to make that happen, God planned some schooling, an *education* for his man, before he could graduate to the throne. Life experiences would be his basic curriculum, and his teacher the Holy Spirit. In this way, David's character would be shaped by his Maker.

David's experience with Abigail was one of the courses God required David to take. But there were some prerequisites to the Abigail encounter. Before you can take advanced algebra, you must take algebra I; before algebra I there is advanced mathematics, and so on. David's prerequisite courses were hard; they were humbling. But as we can see in retrospect, they were essential and benefited David greatly. They would help make him the greatest king of Israel ever.

It was long before David met Abigail that the Lord taught David valuable lessons—lessons about the Lord, about himself, and about others. Before we can fully appreciate the story of Abigail and David, we must look at David's prior experiences. And before his experiences, his difficult life station.

NOT EVEN THE RUNT OF THE LITTER

He was the youngest of eight boys.[1] We are given names for six of them: Eliab, Abinadab, Shimea, Nethanel, Raddai, and Ozem,[2] but the seventh male sibling is not named, remaining a mystery man. David also had two sisters, Zeruiah and Abigail (not our Abigail), and perhaps more.

There is some evidence that Jesse, David's father, and David's seven older brothers, had little respect for the baby of the family. When Samuel came to Jesse's farm surreptitiously to anoint a successor to the failed King Saul, the elderly prophet told Jesse to bring his sons out so that he could review each of them. It does not appear from scripture that Samuel revealed the purpose of his mission, but Jesse did as he was told—except in one minor respect. He didn't include his youngest son, David.

In First Samuel 16, Samuel's meeting with Jesse and his family is recorded in some detail. Jesse and the older boys had assigned David the chore of watching the sheep when Samuel came.[3] The older ones felt that they had more important matters at hand, so important that it was none of David's business. David was shunned from the family's meeting with Samuel, from the sacrifice and meal, and from a consecration ceremony, which Samuel administered, for his older brothers. Apparently, Samuel consecrated the seven as a group, since he was confident that it would be one of these seven that the Lord would tell him to anoint as future king. But Samuel did not even know about David at this point because Jesse hadn't included him or even mentioned the youngster. David was an afterthought. He was all alone, out tending livestock, while his family feasted with Samuel.

So at least for that day's purposes, his own father did not consider David to be a member of the family. Like his many generations later grandson Jesus, David was despised. He was the stone that the builders rejected.[4] And like Jesus, his own family distanced themselves from him.[5] He wasn't even worth mentioning.

Scripture doesn't tell us anything about his feelings, but can you imagine how this must have hurt young David? Jesse hadn't formally told David "I hereby disown you." It was worse than that. Jesse didn't even mention

1. 1 Sam 16:10-11.

2. 1 Chr 2:13-14.

3. 1 Sam 16:11.

4. Ps 118:22.

5. "And when [Jesus'] family heard it, they went out to seize him, for they were saying, 'He is out of his mind.'" Mark 3:21.

him. He ignored his own son. Doesn't Dad claim me anymore? Don't I matter even a little? It surely was a knife to David's heart.

To his family, David was the "runt of the litter"—the pup who can't keep up, the kid who can't compete. But they treated him worse than a runt. They treated him as though he didn't exist. Out in the field. Forgotten. His father, on that day, forsook his son.

GOD REMEMBERED DAVID

But there was another, better, and more lasting family for David. He would later write:

> For my father and my mother have forsaken me,
> but the LORD will take me in.[6]

Perhaps David was recalling the day of Samuel's visit when he wrote Psalm 27. It fits well, because on that day his family did forsake him. But he recalls something else that happened: the Lord, through Samuel, "took me in." Somehow, his Heavenly Father let him know that he wasn't forgotten, that he was part of a far better family, one that would last forever, one that loved him unconditionally, one that honored him as son and brother, one that did not leave him out in the field but noticed him and wanted him to succeed. *That* family would take him in.

At the beginning of this chapter, we noted that God's curriculum for David included lessons about God and lessons about others. Here David learned both. Others—even family—would forsake him; they would fail. Thus he could never take ultimate refuge in man. But he also learned that God would never forsake him. "It is better," he observed, "to take refuge in the LORD than to trust in man."[7] It is better to take refuge in the LORD than to take refuge in your own father!

This was a bedrock truth that would serve David well throughout his life. Of course, he would depend on others, for example, to carry out his orders when he became king. But he would never take *refuge* in anyone other than his God.

---

6. Ps 27:10.

7. Ps 118:8. David also wrote: "[F]or you have been my refuge, a strong tower against the enemy. Let me dwell in your tent forever! Let me take refuge under the shelter of your wings!" (Ps 61:3-4).

GOD HUMBLED DAVID

Jesse and seven of his sons humiliated David by counting him out of the family. Perhaps Jesse's failure to mention David was unintentional, but nevertheless, the family hurt him. They abused him. And God let it happen, but for David's good.

It is fortunate that Samuel pursued the matter. He did so because, prior to his visit, the Lord had told him that the future king would be one of Jesse's sons.[8] Jesse may have made a mistake, but Samuel knew that God hadn't. Because of his confidence in what God had told him, Samuel figured that something didn't add up. It was simple logic: God said the king was one of Jesse's boys; it's none of these seven; you must have another son lurking around here somewhere. Go get him.

Unlike David's seven older brothers, God does not humiliate his sons and daughters. He often subjects them to humiliation by others, as in David's case, but he himself does not humiliate. Intentional humiliation of another is abuse. God does not abuse his children, but he can use the infliction of humiliation by others to make his children *humble*. That is what he was doing with David. He would bring eternal good out of this transient evil.

From birth to death, God humbles his children. This is because he hates pride; he "opposes the proud but gives grace to the humble."[9] The proud will "come to a dreadful end and shall be no more forever"[10] but "[t]he meek shall inherit the earth."[11] Jesus himself, creator of the universe, was humble: "Behold, your king is coming to you . . . humble and mounted on a donkey."[12]

God typically works humility in us through hard experiences. For David, the day of Samuel's visit to Jesse's farm was such a hard experience. On that day, David was being severely humbled, and this shaping of character stuck. Throughout his life David would prove to be a humble man. In this regard he was truly a "man after God's own heart."[13] He, like Jesus, was "meek

8. "The LORD said to Samuel, 'How long will you mourn for Saul, since I have rejected him as king over Israel? Fill your horn with oil and be on your way; I am sending you to Jesse of Bethlehem. I have chosen one of his sons to be king'" (1 Sam 16:1, NIV).

9. Jas 4:6b.

10. Ez 28:19.

11. Ps 37:11; Matt 5:5.

12. Zech 9:9.

13. 1 Sam 13:14.

and lowly in heart"[14] despite his occasional bouts with pride. He instantly accepted Nathan's rebuke regarding his sin with Bathsheba.[15] If he had been proud, he likely would have had the prophet beheaded for insolence.

David also humbly and repeatedly honored Saul as king, even to the point of protecting him from harm when Saul was trying to capture and kill him. And unlike Saul, who arrogantly followed his own counsel, David "inquired of the LORD" before commanding his troops to attack an enemy, not trusting his own wisdom.[16] David had plenty of missteps, but humility was an early lesson and one well learned.

When I was a seminary student, about 30 years old, I was asked to teach a Sunday school class on the book of Romans. There were approximately 25 adults in the class. One Sunday afternoon I began to think about each member of the class and found to my surprise that in my mind I was "dissing" every one of them. Then I asked myself why, because I knew that such an attitude was way out of step with the Lord. Of course, the root of the problem was pride. In every case, as I reviewed my critical evaluation of each person in the class, I could see that what I was really doing was comparing that person to myself—and I wasn't being exactly objective in the process. I shouldn't have been running comparisons anyway, but in doing so I was subconsciously trying to convince myself that I came out on top in every case. It was pride, pure and simple. I repented of it, but that didn't delete it from my character. God has had to continue his work in me through hard, humbling times. I suspect most Christians have had similar experiences.

Humility is a lesson that God, one way or another, teaches all believers. We cannot strut into the Kingdom of Heaven. David began to learn that early on, and it helped make him into the kind of man Abigail would encounter.

DAVID MEETS BEAR AND LION

The children's Bible school song goes: "Little David was a shepherd boy / He killed Goliath and he shouted for joy!" True enough. But before he was able to kill the giant and shout for joy, God had to give him another lesson.

14. Matt 11:29.
15. 2 Sam 12:1–13.
16. E.g., 1 Chr 10:13–14; 1 Sam 23:1.

It was in two parts: the bear part and the lion part. We could say that they were the two semesters of God's physical training curriculum.

It is only in retrospect that we are told of David's confrontation with these killer beasts. David used what he had learned from these encounters when he was making his case before King Saul that he would be able to face Goliath:

> Your servant used to keep sheep for his father. And when there came a lion, or a bear, and took a lamb from the flock, I went after him and struck him and delivered it out of his mouth. And if he arose against me, I caught him by his beard and struck him and killed him. Your servant has struck down both lions and bears, and this uncircumcised Philistine shall be like one of them, for he has defied the armies of the living God.[17]

Boys are not known for killing bears, but bears are known for killing boys. In Second Kings the Bible records an unusual bit of history from the life of the prophet Elisha:

> [Elisha] went up from there to Bethel, and while he was going up on the way, some small boys came out of the city and jeered at him, saying, "Go up, you bald head!" And he turned around, and when he saw them, he cursed them in the name of the LORD. And two she-bears came out of the woods and tore forty-two of the boys.[18]

The boy David faced the bear one-on-one. He accomplished what forty-two boys could not. Was David forty-two times stronger, that much braver? David stated the facts to Saul. He indeed had been the boy who was able to overcome a lion and a bear. But he didn't credit himself. In his conversation with King Saul, he continued,

> The LORD who delivered me from the paw of the lion and from the paw of the bear will deliver me from the hand of this Philistine.[19]

We don't know when it first dawned upon David in his young life that the Lord was his deliverer, but he surely knew it after he killed the bear and the lion! He knew that he was just a kid and that he had not accomplished these feats in his own strength. Yet *he* had been the one who killed the bear. Thus it was that he learned that it is God who brings

17. 1 Sam 17:34–36.
18. 2 Kgs 2:23–24.
19. 1 Sam 17:37a.

the victory, usually bringing it through his servants. He can even bring mighty victories through little shepherd boys.

David now knew this not merely in his head, stored away there as a theological truth. He now knew it in his heart, he felt it in his very being, in his legs and biceps. Having that experience in his past, he could now tell Saul that *he*, David, could go out and face the giant Goliath. *He* could do it because he wouldn't be out there all by himself. The God of Israel, David's only hope and salvation, would be right there with him and help him:

> The LORD is my light and my salvation;
>   whom shall I fear?
> The LORD is the stronghold of my life;
>   of whom shall I be afraid?
> When evildoers assail me
>   to eat up my flesh,
>   my adversaries and foes,
>   it is they who stumble and fall.[20]

THE GIANT

This was a lesson well learned when David met the bear and lion, but David was going for his master's degree when God turned it up a notch with Goliath. I've wondered what was going through David's mind before he ran out onto the field of battle to take on this monster. Perhaps he had a conversation something like this with the Lord:

The LORD: Are you ready, David?

DAVID: All but for my weapon. I couldn't use the armor they gave me because it was too heavy. Besides, I just wasn't used to it. I do have my sling shot, if that'll work.

The LORD: Yes, that will work. Good choice.

DAVID: Haven't got any stones though. Let me get some from the brook over there.

The LORD: Good. Sure. You'll need only one.

DAVID: I'd feel better if I had five or so.

---

20. Ps 27:1-2.

The LORD: Fine, but you'll only use one of them. I'm the best shot in the universe, and I'll be right there with you. Seriously, you'll only need one stone, because *I'll be with you.*

DAVID: I know you'll be with me!—but still . . .

The LORD: No, you can take five stones. Not a problem. But after today you'll see why I said you'd need only one.

David, like all believers, was on a learning curve. He didn't learn everything in one lesson. We humans aren't made to learn or do everything in one class period, so God gives us time and room to grow. "I believe; help my unbelief!"[21] We need *continuing* education. But the important thing to see is that David consistently grew, just as we grow, bit by bit.

David learned that "the LORD is on my side as my helper"[22] progressively, from the tussles with a bear and a lion, from the black day on the farm when Samuel came to visit, up through his confrontation with Goliath, and thereafter. A lesson well learned, but one that David forgot for a spell just before he met Abigail.

QUESTIONS FOR THOUGHT

1. As you think back over your life, can you see a pattern of "education"? That is, can you see ways in which God trained you? Do you think you have progressed?

2. David was enabled to conquer a bear, a lion and a giant. Have you had times when you, like David, were given the strength to do something that you know you couldn't have done on your own?

3. Have you had an experience where someone humiliated you? Though hurtful at the time, can you see any long-term benefits to it?

21. Mark 9:24.
22. Ps 118:7.

2. PROFESSOR SAUL

I n spring the rains come to Missouri and our patchy St. Louis lawn begins to beckon. It wants to be mowed, and I oblige by retrieving the mower from its winter quarters, our backyard shed, and try to start it. For forty years after its winter hibernation, it hasn't started on the first, second or even the tenth pull of the cord, but the years have gone by and I have never given up—that is, I have never learned. This year is no different; persistence has failed me once again so I retrieve my trusty can of starting fluid from the garage and spray it into the air intake. I yank the cable just once again and bang! The mower roars to life—but only for a second or two. Just that quickly, it has run out of starting fluid.

SAUL'S RAPID DECLINE

Saul's reign was much like that. It started off with a bang and a roar, but just that quickly ran out of starting fluid. Samuel anointed him as Israel's first king[1] in about 1020 B.C., and on that very day, when Saul "turned his back" to Samuel to leave, "the Spirit of God rushed upon him, and he prophesied among the prophets."[2] Saul's first foray onto the battlefield was a smashing success when once again "the Spirit of God rushed on him"[3] and he brought Israel a great victory over the Ammonites. He gave thanks to the Lord for the victory and led the men of Israel in worship. But from then on he faltered.

1. 1 Sam 10:1ff.
2. 1 Sam 10:10b.
3. 1 Sam 11:6ff.

His first recorded failure is set out in First Samuel 13. Samuel had instructed Saul to wait for him so that Samuel could offer a burnt offering prior to taking the field against the Philistines. When Samuel didn't show up in accordance with Saul's timetable, Saul couldn't wait it out. He saw some of his troops leaving camp and rather than presenting his predicament to the Lord in prayer, he began to worry, concerned that he wouldn't have enough soldiers left for the march on Philistia. From a merely human standpoint this was not unreasonable, but Saul had learned from Samuel what God's point of view was. Saul had a different point of view and preferred to resort to his own devices. So he took it upon himself to offer the sacrifice, ostensibly to gain the Lord's favor.

But Samuel arrived and rebuked Saul. "You have done foolishly," Samuel told him, and therefore "your kingdom shall not continue. The LORD has sought out a man after his own heart, and the LORD has commanded him to be prince over his people, because you have not kept what the LORD commanded you."[4]

It is important for us to recognize Saul's propensity in ourselves. Often,—no, almost *always*—it seems to us that the Lord shows up late. My checking account is just over $900, and I start to pray, knowing that my monthly bills even at that point exceed $900. The balance slips to $600, then $400. Some of the depletion is due to automatic withdrawals, over which I have no immediate control. Already nervous about what's going to happen, my garbage disposal breaks down. The balance is now $300. My prayers become more earnest. Now it's down to $100, and I turn desperate. This is a crisis, and God doesn't seem to be showing up, though I am praying fervently. He and I seem to have different clocks. And doesn't he care about the disposal?

God and Saul had different clocks too. Saul's had already chimed. He knew that he was supposed to wait for Samuel to offer the sacrifice, but that command was given before his infantry started to leave him, weakening the corps just as they were about to engage the Philistines in battle. What to do? Saul decided to look at his own clock, just as we are tempted to do. Rather than look up, we continue to look around, at our men deserting, at our checkbook closing in on zero.

This is a good time to remember what Saul should have done, but didn't. As scary as the circumstances may be, we need to *wait* for Samuel, that is,

4. 1 Sam 13:14–15.

for God, to act. And he will act. This is the God that the songwriter Dorothy Coates said may not come when you want him to, but he's right on time!

SAUL LACKED FAITH

Not only did Saul disobey Samuel when he offered the sacrifice, but he demonstrated callous disregard for God's promises to him. Before Saul took the throne, the Lord had informed him, through Samuel, that he would "save my people from the hand of the Philistines" and "from the hand of [Israel's] surrounding enemies."[5] These were precious promises from the God of Israel to Saul, but the man treated them like junk mail when he took it upon himself to offer a premature sacrifice on his own. He scuttled God's promise, and did things in his earthly way, on his time-table. He substituted his own judgment for God's. He didn't believe that God would be "right on time."

With the help of Saul's son Jonathan, as well as Saul's then understudy David, God's promises to Saul were indeed accomplished[6] (his promises never fail), but Saul's victories proved to be relatively short lived. His basic problem was that his heart was not right before the Lord.

Later, through Samuel, God commissioned Saul to undertake a mission against the Amalekites. The specific reason for the mission is provided for us, and it had to do with something that had occurred almost 400 years earlier. The Lord instructed Samuel to tell Saul,

> I noted what Amalek did to Israel in opposing them on the way when they came up out of Egypt. Now go and strike Amalek and devote to destruction all that they have. Do not spare them, but kill both man and woman, child and infant, ox and sheep, camel and donkey.[7]

Saul assembled 210,000 of Israel's foot soldiers and soundly defeated Amalek, killing all the Amalekites save one:

> Saul and the people spared Agag [king of Amalek] and the best of the sheep and of the oxen and of the fattened calves and the lambs,

---

5. 1 Sam 9:16b; 1 Sam 10:1b.
6. 1 Sam 14:47ff.
7. 1 Sam 15:2b–3.

and all that was good, and would not utterly destroy them. All that was despised and worthless they devoted to destruction.[8]

Clearly, Saul's reluctance to destroy everyone and everything was not motivated by humanitarian concerns, for he killed every man, woman and child, but spared the king. What he was interested in was the booty: sheep, oxen, fattened calves and lambs. His motivation for sparing Agag was clearly his pride: he wanted a trophy to show off his prowess as a military leader. His preservation of the choice livestock as well as Agag was blatantly disobedient to the Lord's commission.

Samuel then confronted Saul, and said:

> Has the LORD as great delight in burnt offerings
> and sacrifices,
> as in obeying the voice of the LORD?
> Behold, to obey is better than sacrifice,
> and to listen than the fat of rams.
> For rebellion is as the sin of divination,
> and presumption is as iniquity and idolatry.
> Because you have rejected the word of the LORD,
> he has also rejected you from being king.[9]

DAVID LEARNED FROM SAUL

A bang and a roar, and then it was over. In the battle with the Amalekites, Saul disobeyed by not carrying out the Lord's clear command. In his earlier disobedience when he offered an unauthorized sacrifice, he was impatient, disobeying Samuel's express directive to wait for him and demonstrating his lack of faith. For the purposes of our study, his impatient disobedience is particularly relevant.

---

8. 1 Sam 15:9.

9. 1 Sam 15:22-23. *See also* Prov 21:3: "To do righteousness and justice is more acceptable to the Lord than sacrifice." In Joshua's conquest of Jericho, Achan did the same, saving valuable things for himself, and not devoting them to destruction, as the Lord had commanded. Achan confessed: ""It is true! I have sinned against the LORD, the God of Israel. This is what I have done. When I saw in the plunder a beautiful robe from Babylonia, two hundred shekels of silver and a bar of gold weighing fifty shekels, I coveted them and took them. They are hidden in the ground inside my tent, with the silver underneath" (Josh 7:21-22, NIV).

Saul *couldn't wait it out.* He had to take matters into his own hands. David surely learned from this; Saul was a sad object lesson in what can happen if impatience prevails. David later wrote:

> Wait on the LORD:
> be of good courage,
> and he shall strengthen thine heart:
> wait, I say, on the LORD.[10]

We might wonder why the Lord had Samuel anoint Saul as the George Washington of Israel knowing that he would disqualify himself so quickly. Maybe this was one of those very, very rare occasions when God made a mistake? But God doesn't make mistakes even on rare occasions. He does, however, do many things that we cannot begin to understand at the time. We may not understand, but as William Cowper wrote, "God is His own interpreter / And He will make it plain."[11] To an extent, we can see from scripture some of God's reasons for allowing Saul's abysmal failures, particularly when we look at his lengthy and stormy relationship with David.

The Lord used Saul in David's life. He used him to teach David some indispensable lessons that would result in David's spiritual growth, that is, his relationship with and dependence upon the Lord. But Saul's mentorship was altogether in the negative.

I once heard a football fan say of his alma mater's team that had just lost a big game, "they put on a great clinic out there on how not to win a football game." There was a good deal of that going on with Saul and David. Throughout his reign, Saul put on a great clinic out there on how not to be king of Israel. David, next generation down, learned from Saul in this way. Watch out! Don't do that. Look what happened to Saul! Saul had unwittingly joined David's faculty, and David would continue learning from Saul's beleaguered reign for at least a decade.

SAUL ON THE PROWL

From David's victory over Goliath up until Saul's death, Saul was intensely jealous of David. To honor him who was so remarkably successful in battle, the women of the land danced in celebration, and sang "Saul has struck

10. Ps 27:14, KJV.
11. Cowper, "God Moves," stanza 6.

down his thousands, and David his ten thousands!"[12] David had the suburban housewife vote locked up, and the polling data favored him 10-1 in that demographic. Saul was enraged. He realized that he couldn't beat David at the voting booth, so he turned to the sword.

From First Samuel 19 on, the Bible records Saul's dark and pointless pursuits of David. Saul once even resorted to terrorism when he killed eighty-five of the Lord's priests at Nob. Saul was paranoid, suspecting them of conspiring with David against him.[13] But though Saul was determined, David was clever prey and consistently avoided capture.

A CAVE CLASSROOM

There were numerous close calls, though. One is recorded in First Samuel 24, a close encounter for both David and Saul. David and his men had hidden themselves from Saul's posse deep inside a cave located in the Wilderness of Engedi. Saul and his men were apparently just outside the mouth of the cave, unaware that David's men were hiding inside. Suddenly Saul had to answer nature's call. Seeing a flashing "men's room" sign above the entrance to the cave, he went in. As Saul was using the facilities, David, surprised at Saul's intrusion, sneaked up on him and trimmed off a piece of his robe. Saul soon left, not knowing that David had a scrap of his garment in hand.

David's lesson in the cave came not so much from Saul as his own conscience, as informed by the Holy Spirit. David was in a perfect position to do Saul in. And his men encouraged him to take advantage:

> And the men of David said to him, "Here is the day of which the
> LORD said to you, 'Behold, I will give your enemy into your hand,
> and you shall do to him as it shall seem good to you.'"[14]

"Boss," they were saying, "this is exactly what we've been waiting for! This is a golden opportunity—one that doesn't come knocking every day. Go for it! It's the right thing to do!" They had wanted David to kill Saul right then and there.

The men even invoked the Lord's name, and a specific promise they believed he had made to David. This was a strong argument. But David

12. 1 Sam 18:7; 21:11b.

13. 1 Sam 22:11-19.

14. 1 Sam 24:4.

answered his men: "The LORD forbid that I should do this thing to my lord, the LORD's anointed, to put out my hand against him, seeing he is the LORD's anointed."[15]

Surely David was tempted to take his men's advice. Arguably, he appeared to have a right to kill Saul, because it would be self-defense, which had been raised as a legal defense before in scripture.[16] Saul was after him that day for the express purpose of killing him.[17] David surely would have been justified in taking Saul's life on that basis alone.

But the men raised a more compelling argument, one that they thought would be even more attractive to David. This pit stop for Saul, wherein he unknowingly had made himself utterly vulnerable to David, even to the point of baring his derriere (Saul literally had been caught with his pants down), was God's doing and God *meant* for David to snuff him out. After all, David (his men could argue), you've been anointed as King of Israel. This could very well be God's providence, his way of making his promise come to fulfillment.

Apart from other considerations, these were good arguments. If they had been followed, it would have put an end to Saul's insane pursuits. More tempting to David and his men was the fact that it would have instantly installed the already-anointed David as king.

But David deferred. He would not "put out his hand" against the Lord's anointed. There in the cave he made a watershed decision: Let God be God. I will not take matters into my own hands. God will give me the kingdom when he is ready to give me the kingdom, and I will not do that which God alone can do. I will not respond in kind to Saul. I will be patient. This is what David was talking about when he wrote: "Wait on the LORD: be of good courage, and he shall strengthen thine heart: wait, I say, on the LORD."[18]

PRECEDENT

Too, there was a bit of strategy that influenced David here. Involved in his thinking was some savvy self-interest. And it was more than self-interest: he was protecting the throne itself, those who would succeed him as king

15. 1 Sam 24:6.

16. Gen 4:16-17.

17. 1 Sam 20:31b.

18. Ps 27:14, KJV.

of Israel. David knew that he was the anointed successor to Saul. He did not want to set a precedent in which the Anointed was fair game, because then when that person took the throne, he would be fair game.

We see David's reasoning again in this regard when Saul was later killed on the battlefield. A young Amalekite came to David and boasted that he had struck Saul with the fatal blow (at Saul's command, he claimed). The young man expected a trophy, or maybe the Congressional Medal of Honor. But he got neither. David asked him: "How is it you were not afraid to put out your hand to destroy the LORD's anointed?"[19] Whereupon, he had the young man executed.

No, David would not set a precedent that allowed a man to kill the one God had anointed, even if that person commanded him to do it. He would not permit another man to do what he had refrained from doing when he was holed up in the cave with his men. One does not put out his hand against the Lord's anointed and escape the consequences.

DAVID CONFRONTS SAUL

After Saul left the cave, David came out following him at a safe distance. Waving the remnant of Saul's robe in the air so that the king and his troops would be sure to see it, David called out to Saul and said:

> See, my father, see the corner of your robe in my hand. For by the fact that I cut off the corner of your robe and did not kill you, you may know and see that there is no wrong or treason in my hands. I have not sinned against you, though you hunt my life to take it. May the LORD judge between me and you, *may the LORD avenge me against you*, but my hand shall not be against you.[20]

David assured Saul that he had nothing to fear from him. Indeed, David made it clear to Saul that he had actually protected him from harm that day, even though David's men had urged him otherwise. But David also lets Saul know that there is One who *will* avenge, someone far more ominous than David. Saul should be concerned about him, not David.

---

19. 2 Sam 1:14.

20. 1 Sam 24:11-12 (emphasis added).

DAVID KNEW HIS BIBLE

Psalm 119 is ample testimony to the fact that David knew his Bible well. For him that was just the Pentateuch, the first five books of our Bible. But even that much of God's Word gave him confidence, there with his men in the cave, that he was making the right decision in not taking Saul's life, for God would deal with Saul. The Lord had guaranteed that he would, and David could rest in that assurance from what Moses said in Deuteronomy:

> Vengeance is mine, and recompense, for the time when their foot shall slip; for the day of their calamity is at hand, and their doom comes swiftly.[21]

David, not Saul, was the one who came away from that encounter relaxed and relieved. Saul's angst was only heightened, because he had just heard David call out to him "*may the* LORD *avenge me against you.*" These were ominous words for Saul, especially since he had just acknowledged David's righteousness and his future ascension to the throne:

> You are more righteous than I . . . may the LORD reward you with good for what you have done to me this day. And now, behold, I know that you shall surely be king, and that the kingdom of Israel shall be established in your hand.[22]

No matter what the state of Saul's heart at the time (he appeared penitent), he nevertheless had to worry that the Lord would do exactly what David had asked, and avenge David against him.

One would think that after this encounter David's mind would be set for life on the matter of leaving vengeance in God's hands. So it is perplexing when we read First Samuel 25, the study of this book. When he encountered Nabal, it seems that David had totally forgotten what he had known so well in the cave.

QUESTIONS FOR THOUGHT

1. Saul's reign began well, but his early successes proved to be a "false start." What is it about Saul that displeased the Lord, so that his blessing upon him was removed? How does Saul differ from David?

---

21. Deut 32:35. *See also* Rom 12:19.
22. 1 Sam 24:17-20.

2. When someone has hurt you, have you said or done something to get back at them? If so, do you still think your reaction was a good idea?

3. Saul couldn't "wait it out." At the present time, are you having to wait something out? Why do you continue to wait, knowing you could do something about it right now? Why do you think God is making you wait?

3. NABAL MEANS FOOL

I f ever there was a motley crew, it was David's band of men. They were a strange mix, and seemingly unfit for hire, particularly for the military. They were made up of "everyone who was in distress, and everyone who was in debt, and everyone who was bitter in soul"[1]—not shining, uniformed young officers recently graduated from West Point. At the start, there were about 400 of them. They attached themselves to David, and he became their commander. They were a scraggly bunch, for sure: maybe some good, but mostly bad and ugly.

David was on the run at the time, hiding in the Cave of Adullum, a stronghold in the southern part of Israel. Saul was after him, and doubtless those more desirable citizens who were *not* in distress, in debt, or bitter in soul, did not feel it safe or prudent to join forces with anyone whom Saul opposed. Upstanding, successful citizens had something to lose. But the motley crew were desperate men and had nothing to lose. So they joined up with David.

David trained his men. He didn't know when he would need them to face Saul or some other opposing force, but though small in number, he expected them to be ready. They possessed dubious abilities at the start, but these men would be part of his standing army, and eventually out of them would come some of David's mighty men.[2]

1. 1 Sam 22:2.
2. 2 Sam 23:8-39.

KEEPING HIS MEN BUSY

After Saul and David left the cave, David and his growing militia moved into the Wilderness of Paran (v.1), also known as the Wilderness of Maon. The troops settled there for a time. Here, between the cities of Maon and Carmel, would be the venue for David's encounter with Abigail.

David was not one for allowing his men to sit on their hands or waste time playing poker or computer games. Twiddling their thumbs in the Wilderness of Paran wouldn't do; the troops needed to keep busy doing something constructive (and hopefully profitable). But what? David scoped out the neighborhood, and found an opportunity:

> And there was a man in Maon whose business was in Carmel. The man was very rich; he had three thousand sheep and a thousand goats. He was shearing his sheep in Carmel. Now the name of the man was Nabal, and the name of his wife Abigail. (vv.2–3a)

David evidently did not approach Nabal to ask permission, but took it upon himself to do what he was particularly good at doing. David had learned the craft in his childhood, taking care of his father's flocks. As we have seen in chapter 1, David learned that shepherding wasn't always idyllic, pastoral or peaceful. Sometimes it meant tangling with a bear or a lion, wild beasts who were dreaming of mutton chops for dinner. It also meant driving off human marauders. David, without asking Nabal first, took up this difficult task, and began guarding Nabal's men who were keeping their master's sheep. David and his men greatly impressed Nabal's servants, for they later told Abigail that "[David's men] were a wall to us both by night and by day, all the while we were with them keeping the sheep" (v.16).

HUNGRY TROOPS AND A REQUEST FOR FOOD

David had heard that Nabal was shearing his sheep, and as was the custom in those days, throwing a party to celebrate the resultant bales of new wool.[3] Alcoholic beverages were flowing. Everyone was in a good mood, it

---

3. Three thousand sheep (v.2) can produce about fifteen tons of new wool annually. Sometimes there are exceptions. One Australian sheep, lost in the woods for five years, carried 80 pounds of wool. His 2021 shearing can be seen here: Sheep Covered In 80 Pounds Of Wool Makes Most Amazing Transformation | The Dodo Faith = Restored - Bing video (accessed 3/15/2023).

seemed, and well-oiled to boot. David thought this would be a perfect time to approach Nabal with a request.

David and his men needed food. Surely, he thought, Nabal will appreciate the work they had performed for his shepherds. Nabal was the direct beneficiary of that work, and one would think he would be happy indeed to show some token of his appreciation. So David sent an entourage of ten young men to the partying Nabal with this message:

> Peace be to you, and peace be to your house, and peace be to all that you have. I hear that you have shearers. Now your shepherds have been with us, and we did them no harm, and they missed nothing all the time they were in Carmel. Ask your young men, and they will tell you. Therefore let my young men find favor in your eyes, for we come on a feast day. Please give whatever you have at hand to your servants and to your son David. (vv.6-8)

Perhaps this seems a presumptuous request. Certainly it was bold. Did David have a *legal* right to compensation? There doesn't appear to have been an agreement by which Nabal was required to pay for services rendered. Absent such an express agreement, no strict legal right existed.

But David's request really was not presumptuous at all. He did have an *equitable* right to compensation. An equitable right does not require an express legal agreement but is essentially "what's fair is fair." This kind of right is of ancient origin and is enforceable in court to this day. It is traceable at least to early Roman law, the principle being that no person should benefit at another's expense. Today the rule of law comes under the rubric of "unjust enrichment."[4] Nabal should not be enriched at David's expense; that would be "unjust." Further, Mosaic law is saturated end to end with the principle of equity in all human dealings, and as noted, David knew Mosaic law well. David had a perfectly valid claim.

However, David wisely did not present the request to Nabal as a legal or equitable right. He approached Nabal in a friendly, gentlemanly manner: "Let my young men find favor in your eyes . . ." In other words, "Could you do me a big favor, Nabal? My men are hot, weary, and hungry after all the work they've done out here in the wilderness for your men. We'd be forever grateful if you'd give us some food!"

---

4. *Black's*: "'Unjust enrichment' is '[t]he general principle that one person should not be permitted unjustly to enrich himself at expense of another, but should be required to make restitution of or for property or benefits received[.]'"

REQUEST SUMMARILY DENIED

Nabal was no gentleman though, nor was he about to respond to a gentleman's request in a gentlemanly manner; it just wasn't in him. *Nabal* is the Hebrew word for "fool," and as Abigail told David later, "Nabal is his name, and folly is with him" (v.25). When Nabal's parents filled out his birth certificate, they hit the nail on the head. Or perhaps "Nabal" wasn't his legal name, but the name by which he was commonly known, due to his behavior.

Nabal lived up to, or down to, his name. He answered David's ten young men:

> Who is David? Who is the son of Jesse? There are many servants these days who are breaking away from their masters. Shall I take my bread and my water and my meat that I have killed for my shearers and give it to men who come from I do not know where? (vv.10–11)[5]

It appears that Nabal had a good deal of practice in the art of insult. As insults go, this one is magnificent. "Who is David?" He knew very well who David was, for he follows with "Who is the son of Jesse?" and the young men hadn't mentioned David's parentage. David had killed the giant Goliath, making the evening news throughout Israel. He was famous—too famous as far as Saul was concerned—and that's the reason Saul was after him. The women of the land sang his praises. Abigail, Nabal's wife, not only knew who David was but also that he would be Saul's successor (v.30). Everyone knew who David was. Nabal was just dissing him, and only a fool would dis a future king. His ignorance regarding David's identity was a pretense. Nabal was digging a hole for himself.

And he dug it deeper (as fools tend to do). He continued, "[t]here are many servants these days who are breaking away from their masters." Nabal is purposely making light of David's separation from Saul, as though David was nothing more than a disgruntled errand-boy sneaking away from his employer, looking for a better job. Of course David wasn't "breaking away from his master" at all. King Saul had driven him from the palace by throwing a spear at him.[6]

Then Nabal proceeds to humiliate David's men. "Shall I take my bread and my water and my meat that I have killed for my shearers and

5. Notice Nabal's evident self-absorption and selfishness: "my bread," "my water," "my meat," and "my shearers."

6. 1 Sam 19:10–12.

give it to men who come from I do not know where?" No you don't, Nabal, and that's not what you are being asked to do. You well know that these are the men who protected your men out there in the wild. You have the meat that you're barbequing for your shearers in large part because of what David's men have done for you.

The now embarrassed and humiliated entourage got the message, left the guffawing Nabal, and retraced their steps to David, still camped out with the rest of his men in the wilderness. They reported Nabal's words to David. His request had been not merely denied, but ridiculed.

DAVID'S RAGING RESPONSE

Clearly, David was not expecting this kind of report from his messengers. He had not made any sort of demand upon Nabal, but only a humble request. He could have expected at least a gracious response, even if the answer was "no."

David was roiled—*really* roiled. "Every man strap on his sword!" he shouted to his cadre (vv.13ff). They did. David strapped his on too. Four hundred armed rangers and their commander, ready to attack. Two hundred (their ranks now having increased to 600) were assigned to stay with the baggage. This was no longer about getting his men something to eat. It was now about *honor*, and it meant war. Nabal, you just don't talk to David like that. Nobody does.

This is just a shade or two different from what we saw a few paragraphs ago, when David penned his friendly memo to Nabal: "Peace be to you, and peace be to your house, and peace be to all that you have." That was before David was acquainted with Nabal. Now he saw him more accurately for what he was: a mean-spirited, ungrateful, surly fool. David was going to clean Nabal's house:

> Surely in vain have I guarded all that this fellow has in the wilderness, so that nothing was missed of all that belonged to him, and he has returned me evil for good. God do so to the enemies of David and more also, if by morning I leave so much as one male of all who belong to him. (vv.21-22)

It's unfortunate that David wasn't under the tutelage of London's great preacher and pastor Charles Haddon Spurgeon during the Nineteenth

Century, because if he had been, Spurgeon would have counseled him like this:

> If, my dear friend, you make it a rule that nobody shall ever insult you without having to pay for it, nor treat you with disrespect without meeting his match, you need not pray God in the morning to help you carry out your resolve.[7]

In other words, Spurgeon would counsel us, you can "carry out your resolve" to avenge yourself, but don't look for God to help you. He won't.

DAVID ACTS OUT OF CHARACTER

Now it's very true that Nabal was brutish, arrogant, dismissive, insulting and whatever other trash adjectives we might conjure up. But the death penalty?—for Nabal and all his men? Have you thought this through, David? Is this good strategy? Is it a wise course of action? Are you being calm, cool and collected?

This appears to be the first time that David planned to strike out on his own, that is, before inquiring of the Lord. Saul did things on his own regularly, but in First Samuel 23 we see what was more characteristic of young David:

> Now they told David, "Behold, the Philistines are fighting against Keilah and are robbing the threshing floors." Therefore David *inquired of the* Lord, "Shall I go and attack these Philistines?" And the Lord said to David, "Go and attack the Philistines and save Keilah."[8]

But in the Nabal episode, David was angry, and here angry means furious, really mad. When you're really mad, reason takes a seat in the back. David was so mad that he forgot what he knew so well in the cave when he had spared Saul's life: "[L]eave it to the wrath of God; . . . vengeance is mine; I will repay, says the Lord."[9]

When a person is over-the-top angry, he is in a precarious state spiritually. God warned Cain of this,[10] but Cain took no heed, and wound

7. Spurgeon, *Metropolitan Tabernacle Pulpit*, 556.

8. 1 Sam 23:1-2 (emphasis added).

9. Deut 32:35; Rom 12:19.

10. Cain was angry because God accepted Abel's sacrifice but not his: "[B]ut for Cain and his offering [God] had no regard. So Cain was very angry, and his face fell. The Lord said to Cain, 'Why are you angry, and why has your face fallen? If you do well, will you

up murdering his brother Abel. The distance between "mad" and murder is only an inch or two, and David was in danger of doing exactly what Cain did.

This was no time for David to be making decisions about the mobilization of troops. He was in danger of leading himself and his troops down a very dangerous and destructive path. He, like Cain, needed to rule over his anger, but he would need someone to come along side of him to help him do so.

ORIGINS OF DAVID'S ANGER

We might wonder where this outburst of rage came from. It was like a volcano, erupting from deep within, and there are reasons. David's anger came from somewhere, and it is instructive to look back, beginning with his early childhood and teenage years. We've seen in chapter 1 how he was treated, as evidenced by the way his father and older brothers ignored him when the prophet Samuel came to visit. As we noticed, this hurt the boy. It was a put-down.

There is evidence, too, that this kind of treatment was a pattern that continued in Jesse's family at least through the Goliath confrontation, and probably after that. David came to the valley where Goliath stood because his father had sent him with some home cooking for three older brothers serving in Saul's army. When David saw the giant, and heard him scoffing at the Israelites and the God of Israel, he asked some of the soldiers, "[W]ho is this uncircumcised Philistine, that he should defy the armies of the living God?"

Big brother Eliab, the oldest, heard what David said, and didn't care for it at all. Nor did he care for his impudent kid brother:

> Now Eliab his eldest brother heard when he spoke to the men. And Eliab's anger was kindled against David, and he said, "Why have you come down? And with whom have you left those few sheep in the wilderness? I know your presumption and the evil of your heart, for you have come down to see the battle." And David said, "What have I done now? Was it not but a word?"[11]

---

not be accepted? And if you do not do well, sin is crouching at the door. Its desire is contrary to you, but you must rule over it'" (Gen 4:6-7).

11. 1 Sam 17:28b-29.

Eliab didn't thank David for the package of parched grain and freshly baked bread that he brought for them. He doesn't even mention it. What he does mention are the sheep that David was leaving unattended (even though their father Jesse had ordered him to take the trip).[12] He calls them a "few" sheep, as if David couldn't handle a whole flock—and this to the one who had killed lions and bears to protect them.

He also assigns bad motives to David: you have come down to watch the battle—the care package is just an excuse. Eliab was chastising David for having hidden, evil motives, which he didn't and which they weren't. They would not have been even if his interest in the battle had been the moving reason for his making the trip. Eliab is haughtily instructing David that battle is for grownups, not kids, and David should shut up and skedaddle back to the farm where he came from, and do what kids do, tend to a handful of sheep out in the wilderness. The whole thing was a put-down.

PATTERN OF ABUSE

Eliab was humiliating David once again, and this time in front of the soldiers. David's response to Eliab speaks volumes. "What have I done now? Was it not but a word?" His question is revealing as to his wretched relationship with the older boys. "What have I done *now*?" says that this kind of treatment was ongoing. "Was it not but a word?" says that he was always being told to keep his mouth shut. Can't I say anything without getting yelled at? The older boys were *always* putting him down, telling him to keep still, and young David was frustrated. He was also getting more than a little annoyed and resentful.

There are horror stories about parents who put their child in a cage for a month to teach them to eat spinach or not to wet the bed. We consider that to be abuse of the worst kind. But such abuse can be inflicted without a steel cage. It happens when a youngster is constantly belittled, derided, mocked and scorned. The child begins to think of himself as a big nothing, worthless, and an embarrassment to the world. He is being consigned to a cage without steel bars, a prison of hopelessness. He may even come to the point of wanting to die; the pain is just too great.[13]

12. David had dutifully appointed a keeper for the sheep before he made the trip: "And David rose early in the morning and left the sheep with a keeper and took the provisions and went, as Jesse had commanded him" (1 Sam 17:20).

13. Jesus reserved some of his most stinging words of judgment for those who so

FALLOUT FROM ABUSE

None of us likes put-downs. They hurt terribly, particularly when they are ongoing and purposely meant to humiliate. There had to be a deep-seated resentment in David's heart. The older brothers wounded David again and again. Their put-downs and lack of respect were abusive, and this kind of abuse has long-term consequences. Personally, I have never been on the receiving end of such put-downs. My older siblings, Julie and Joel, were very different from Eliab. Even in my errors—which were many—my siblings constantly encouraged me, and even bragged on me to others. They never once shamed me in front of others, but rather advanced my cause. Brothers and sisters should do that, but Eliab did the opposite.

We should not be shocked at David's reaction to Nabal's colossal put-down. It tore open an old fissure, and red-hot lava came spewing out. Perhaps this doesn't excuse David's explosion when he got Nabal's message, but it helps to explain it. Nabal had pushed the "put-down" button which had been pushed too many times before. The subsequent eruption didn't come from nowhere; it had been simmering in David for years.

YOUNG MAN UNDER PRESSURE

David's age, too, probably had something to do with his outburst. He was still in his twenties because he was only thirty when he took the throne. He was not yet the mature, seasoned general he would become. He might have been better off to do what Anthony McAuliffe, senior United States officer with the 101st Airborne Division, did during the Battle of the Bulge in late 1944. When the Germans demanded an "honorable surrender" of Bastogne, McAuliffe sent back a now famous one-word written response: "NUTS!" David, if he responded to Nabal at all, should have done the same: "My dear Nabal—NUTS!" rather than shouting "Every man strap on his sword!" But he was young and mad, like gasoline and a match. He wasn't keeping things in perspective.

In defense of David, we should remember some of the mitigating circumstances. Adverse circumstances coming at the same time from more than one direction can produce a perfect storm. David had just said that

---

offend the young: "But whoso shall offend one of these little ones which believe in me, it were better for him that a millstone were hanged about his neck, and that he were drowned in the depth of the sea" (Matt 18:6, KJV).

Saul was pursuing him like a "dead dog."[14] David had to worry night and day that Saul would show up to kill him. He had that continuous nightmarish pressure on one end, and now a fool on the other. He had done a good deed by protecting Nabal's men. He and his men were worn out. They had stayed up days and nights on end protecting Nabal's men.[15] Now he makes a polite request for food for his band of hungry men and not only is the request denied, but he and his men are personally berated in the process. Where was God in all this? Satan was more visible to David than God. He felt between the devil and the deep blue sea, and it seemed too much for a man to handle. It's not surprising that he got mad. David was human.

SATAN THE OPPORTUNIST

Satan, of course, was in the room. He had been in the cave, too, but David resisted him successfully. Satan doesn't give up, and what an "opportune time"[16] this was to tempt David, God's chosen heir to the throne! The roaring lion was on the prowl.[17] He was much more dangerous than the lions David had conquered while tending sheep. Satan knew that he had failed to trap David into killing Saul in the cave, so, as with Jesus, Satan was looking for another opportunity. David was vulnerable to his wiles. David hadn't taken vengeance against Saul, but Saul was still pursuing him. "Maybe," Satan whispers, "now is a time when you *should* take vengeance. Your decision not to kill Saul sure hasn't done you any good, has it? Go ahead and get mad. Vent. Nabal had no right to talk to you like that. Kill the fool! It'll make you feel better."

To an extent, David succumbed. He got mad, and for a time probably luxuriated in venting. It can feel good for a moment. But when you're mad, you're in a rush, and don't take the time to think things through. Nor do you take time to inquire of the Lord, that is, to pray. Strap on the swords first and pray later. Many of us suffer from this syndrome. And the rush

14. At the cave confrontation, David called out to Saul, "After whom has the king of Israel come out? After whom do you pursue? After a dead dog! After a flea!" (1 Sam 24:14).

15. "They were a wall to us both by night and by day, all the while we were with them keeping the sheep" (v.16).

16. Jesus faced the same, after he had been tempted by Satan in the wilderness: "And when the devil had ended every temptation, he departed from him until an opportune time" (Luke 4:13).

17. 1 Pet 5:8.

in this case was generated by David alone, not Nabal. Though Nabal had insulted David, his men weren't on the attack. But David set a deadline: his terrorist attack was to be carried out before the sun came up the next day. David's intended action was wrong at the outset because he didn't ask God for guidance. He was in too much of a rush.

In failing to inquire of the Lord, David was doing what Eve did in the first transgression. Of course, Adam and Eve did not need to inquire of God because he had already informed them that they must not eat of the Tree of the Knowledge of Good and Evil. Their eating of the fruit was in blatant disobedience to what God had told them. But in her sin, Eve substituted herself for God, and David was about to do the same. David and Eve were both saying to God, in essence, "Give me the keys. I'll drive. In this case my judgment is superior to yours." Whenever a person tries to "take the keys" out of God's hand, they are headed for a wreck.[18]

IT'S ALL ABOUT ME

There were other reasons that David's plan was wrong. It was all about David, not Israel, not the Lord. He was thinking only about himself when he said, "God do so to the enemies of David and more also, if by morning I leave so much as one male of all who belong to him" (v.22). He meant to make a resounding statement to Nabal and everyone else in the immediate vicinity, "Don't mess with me. I'm *David*, the future king!"

I'm sure all of us have been acquainted with people who sometimes act like this. I witnessed it in a senior partner I had in the early days of my law practice. I'll call him "Ted Z—." Ted was a gifted trial lawyer and taught me much, but he could be pompous about his ability. One afternoon I overheard him on the phone talking to the opposing attorney as both were attempting to settle a case coming up for trial the next week. They were nowhere near agreement. Ted was shouting into the phone, "Don't you know who you're talking to? I'm Ted Z—, and I'm going to mop up the courtroom floor with you next week!" That did not play well with the other lawyer, and not with me either. A man makes a fool of himself when

18. We might also note that in God's plan of redemption, he has turned the tables on us in a wonderful way. Eve substituted herself for God, thus plunging all of humankind into sin and warfare against God. But in his mercy, to bring about a perfect redemption, God did the reverse, substituting himself for humankind. (See Stott, *The Cross of Christ*, chapter six.)

he talks like that. But David was saying the same thing: "Nabal, I'm going to mop up the floor with you before tomorrow morning. Don't you know who you're talking to?"

HOW TO HANDLE A FOOL

Solomon, David's son, would say that his father wasn't being "prudent" in his response to Nabal's insult. He wrote:

> The vexation of a fool is known at once,
> but the prudent ignores an insult.[19]

David's temper had blocked out good judgment. He should have done what the Apostle Peter counseled believers to do: "For this is the will of God, that *by doing good* you should put to silence the ignorance of foolish people."[20] For the moment, David wasn't planning on "doing good." He was planning on doing evil. His plan was to put to silence the ignorance of a foolish person by killing him. But this, in and of itself, was foolish. David wanted to teach Nabal a lesson by killing him. I have always wondered (at least from age eight) about what lesson can be taught, or how much can be learned, through the death of the 'student.'

When I was eight or so, our family lived on a bumpy, dusty gravel road in rural eastern Iowa. Our farmer neighbors to the north had a dog "Butch" who was the kids' favorite. He was friendly, smart, and fun to play with. However, he had one bad habit: chasing passing vehicles on the gravel road. I don't believe he ever caught one or would have known what to do with it if he had (Butch couldn't drive), but that didn't diminish his enthusiasm.

One summer day his cheerful fervor for the sport led to his untimely demise. When an over-the-weight-limit truck approached, Butch shot out into the dusty road in hopes that this time he might get the best of the truck. But the truck got the best of Butch. We kids all went out on the roadway and tried to comfort our friend and playmate with soothing words, but he had departed his earthly journey.

Our neighbors had a pretty, fiery-red-headed five-year-old daughter, Mary Sue. She, like all of us, was huddled over the dog. She was crying, smoothing Butch's brow lovingly. When it became clear that the poor dog had expired, she stood up, wiped the tears from her eyes, pointed at the late

19. Prov 12:16.
20. 1 Pet 2:15 (emphasis added).

Butch and said "Well, *that'll* teach him!" Both David and Mary Sue, we might say, were barking up the wrong tree. Any lesson that Butch or Nabal might have learned wasn't going to do *them* any good—at least not in this life.

INNOCENT BYSTANDERS

David was also painting with too broad a brush. Even if Nabal deserved to be done in (which he didn't, at least not by David's hand), his men certainly did not. Indeed, some of his men boasted about David and his efforts on their behalf; they were actually on his side:

> But one of [Nabal's] young men told Abigail, Nabal's wife, "Behold, David sent messengers out of the wilderness to greet our master, and he railed at them. Yet the men were very good to us, and we suffered no harm, and we did not miss anything when we were in the fields, as long as we went with them. They were a wall to us both by night and by day, all the while we were with them keeping the sheep." (vv.14-16)

This young man, an advocate for David and his men, would have been swept away with the rest of Nabal's men if David's plan had been carried out. David should have been more discriminating before giving his broadside command. His attack would have been grossly unjust, something that should be abhorrent to the future king of Israel. And it would have been abhorrent to David if he had taken time to think and pray.

DAVID RISKED FOOLISHNESS AND MURDER

Notice too that David's temper was about to make a fool out of *him*. Solomon, David's son, wrote, "Answer not a fool according to his folly, lest you be like him yourself."[21] Responding to a fool as David planned to do was about to make a fool out of David. In his anger, he didn't comprehend that. When he was in his right mind, he knew better, as demonstrated by his continued refusal to respond in kind to Saul. But unreasoning fury had clean ejected all of that from his brain for the moment.

David's planned attack amounted to nothing other than rank terror. It was eerily similar to Saul's attack on the priests of Nob, recorded in First Samuel 22. There, as mentioned previously, Saul put eighty-five of the

---

21. Prov 26:4.

Lord's appointed priests to death on a trumped-up charge of conspiracy against the Crown. David didn't recognize now how much like Saul he was about to become.

Worst of all, though, was that David had a *plan*. When you plan to kill someone, it's premeditated. Premeditated killing of another is Murder One. In our times David could have been charged with multiple counts of first-degree murder, one count for murdering Nabal and one for each of his servants.

David was about to become a mass murderer, a fool like Nabal and a terrorist like Saul. Someone needed to intervene—and quickly—because David and his men meant to finish the job before sunup.

QUESTIONS FOR THOUGHT

1. The Bible says that Nabal was a "fool." Can you remember other instances where the term is used in the Bible? Based on that, can you come up with a good working definition of the word?

2. Everyone has been insulted. Think of an insult that you've received. How did you react? Are you happy that you reacted the way you did, or do you wish you could go back in time and redo it?

3. When you've gotten really, really angry at someone, have you ever wanted, even for a split second, to do them in? Or that someone would do it on your behalf? Assuming you didn't follow through on your impulse, did your getting mad feel good? Did it help you in the long term?

4. ABIGAIL

A bigail was "discerning and beautiful" but married to Nabal who was "harsh and badly behaved . . ." (v.3b). We have already seen in the previous chapter what kind of man Nabal was. Considering that, to describe him as "harsh and badly behaved" may seem to be giving him a light sentence, but we will stick to what the Bible says.

One might wonder at the outset how it was that an intelligent, discerning woman wound up marrying such a meanspirited dolt. Perhaps she was very young at the time and didn't see Nabal for what he was. Perhaps she married him for the money because it is true that "the man was very rich" (v.2). That, however, would have been most unwise and she was intelligent and discerning. It is more likely that the marriage was arranged, and she had no choice in the matter. If it was arranged, those who put it together probably did so hoping that some of Nabal's shekels would come rolling their way. Whatever the case, for good or for evil, Nabal and Abigail were man and wife—but *only* "until death do us part," which in this case, as we shall see, turned out to be a valuable escape clause!

ABIGAIL GIVEN THE NEWS

As set out in the previous chapter, Abigail heard of David's rash plan from one of Nabal's servants:

> But one of the young men told Abigail, Nabal's wife, "Behold, David sent messengers out of the wilderness to greet our master, and he railed at them. Yet the men were very good to us, and we suffered no harm, and we did not miss anything when we were

in the fields, as long as we went with them. They were a wall to us both by night and by day, all the while we were with them keeping the sheep. Now therefore know this and consider what you should do, for harm is determined against our master and against all his house, and he is such a worthless man that one cannot speak to him." (vv.14-17)

There is some mystery here. David planned a surprise attack under cover of darkness. It was to be completed before sunup. Surely this information was in the file folder stamped "top secret," yet Nabal's servants found out about it. Someone had spilled the beans, and it surely wasn't David. Someone had told Nabal's servants that David had sworn to kill Nabal *and all his servants* by this time tomorrow. The servants' lives were at stake. They too needed immediate intervention.

SECURITY BREACH

It is most likely that at least some of David's men knew that their boss's plan was crazy, that David was presently unhinged. They couldn't approach David right now because of his state of mind; he had temporarily become somewhat like Nabal in that respect. So what to do in such an emergency? They knew they were taking a huge risk and opening themselves to a possible court-martial for treason under David's version of the Uniform Code of Military Justice, but they had to tell someone.

David's and Nabal's servants had become friends out there in the wilderness. Clearly Nabal's men respected David's men: "they were a wall to us" (v.16). Remember, as mentioned in chapter 3, that these were once society's dropouts: "everyone who was in distress, and everyone who was in debt, and everyone who was bitter in soul."[1] David's training program transformed them so that Nabal's men could now describe them as a veritable wall of protection.

So the two bands of men by this time weren't strangers. It is most reasonable to conclude that David's servants confided in Nabal's servants, telling them what David planned to do. Both "sides" recognized that David's servants would have to obey their commander's orders, but both also saw it as imperative that someone intervene, someone who could put a stop to this nonsense.

1. 1 Sam 22:2.

This was not at all because they wanted to protect Nabal, but because they were looking out for David's welfare as well as their own. It appears that no one mentioned in First Samuel 25 was much interested in protecting Nabal.

APPEAL TO ABIGAIL

The enlisted men on both sides in this conflagration appear to have had more common sense than their commanding officers. Nabal's servant had to do something immediately, because David's order was urgent. The young man needed someone who would carry some weight in the matter. So he turned to Abigail, which says something about this amazing woman. The servants knew that Abigail had the good sense that her husband lacked. Apparently, they also knew that she was courageous because intervention between a drunken fool and a madman carried great risk, a risk that the servants did not wish to take on their own.

Time was of the essence. The servant was direct with Abigail: "Now therefore know this and consider what you should do" (v.17a). He also must have known that Abigail had little respect for her husband, because he rather easily recites a fact that he knew Abigail would agree with: "He is such a worthless man that one cannot speak to him" (v.17b). He wasn't telling her anything she didn't already know; it was the opinion of the whole household, and probably the entire community.

ABIGAIL'S INSTANTANEOUS RESPONSE

The servant advised Abigail to "consider what you should do," and she did:

> Then Abigail made haste and took two hundred loaves and two skins of wine and five sheep already prepared and five seahs of parched grain and a hundred clusters of raisins and two hundred cakes of figs, and laid them on donkeys. And she said to her young men, "Go on before me; behold, I come after you." But she did not tell her husband Nabal. And as she rode on the donkey and came down under cover of the mountain, behold, David and his men came down toward her, and she met them. (vv.18-20)

Abigail knew that David's men needed food, and in a blink she put together a feast. She didn't have time to go to the Carmel A&P first, nor did

44

she need to, for Nabal had unwittingly prepared more than David's men could eat. He had mentioned the already-prepared meal when he shot his insulting missive back at David: "Shall I take my bread and my water and my meat that I have killed for my shearers and give it to men who come from I do not know where?" (v.11).

Abigail is going to do just that. Nabal and his shearers would have to do without, at least to the extent of *two hundred loaves of fresh bread and two kegs of wine and five sheep already prepared and five seahs of parched grain and a hundred clusters of raisins and two hundred cakes of figs!* But they and their boss were liquored up, so that their eyes were bleary. They didn't notice that their food supply was being substantially depleted by the mistress of the house. Thus, it isn't a surprise that Abigail was able to keep all this a secret from Nabal.

ON THE ROAD

Abigail then had Nabal's servants load the huge catered spread on some of his donkeys, the delivery vans of the day, taking an extra donkey for her own transport. She and her caravan stealthily left the farm for a visit with David, with the donkey train and her servants in the lead. Abigail and her donkey brought up the rear.

This took great courage. Here she was, wife of the very man David meant to kill, ready to take up the matter in dispute with the avowed enemy of her entire household. But she came armed with food, which was crucial because that is what David had asked Nabal to provide in the first place. And David had asked him only for "whatever you have at hand," but she was bringing that times ten.

A HOUSE GIFT

Abigail's bringing a present calls to mind other places in Scripture where the strategy was used successfully. One such is when Jacob sent his sons from famine-struck Canaan to Egypt on a second trip to buy food. All of them knew that there could be problems because of what happened to them on the first trip: the lord of the land (Joseph) had ordered them to bring Benjamin with them on their next trip, which Jacob vigorously opposed. But they had no choice if they were to have something to eat. Jacob finally relented and told them: "If it must be so, then do this: take some of the choice fruits of the land in your bags, and carry a present down to the man, a little balm and a little honey, gum, myrrh, pistachio nuts, and almonds."[2]

Jacob did the same when he was about to meet up with his estranged brother Esau.[3] Doing this signifies good will, friendship, and cordiality. The same thing is true today when we take a house gift along on a visit, although I can't recall ever doing that where the lives of my family were at stake.

Here, although Abigail at some point had more than an inkling as to what David's reaction might be to her and to what she had to say (as we shall see), she was going to give him what he asked for in the first place and was demonstrating her good will in the process. A dozen or so donkeys loaded with much-needed food at least wouldn't hurt.

AN ATTRACTIVE MESSENGER

Perhaps it goes without saying, but Abigail's beauty didn't exactly hamper her venture. We know it is relevant because the Bible mentions her appearance. The text describes her as "discerning and beautiful" (v.3b) and for a reason. At the risk of being accused of sexism, I will state a fact that everyone knows to be true anyway: a beautiful woman can be beguiling and captivating. God can use beauty, together with anything else he wants, to accomplish his plans.

But a woman must be more than pretty to argue a case. If she proves to have no wisdom, no discretion, her beauty can backfire. Solomon wrote, "Like a gold ring in a pig's snout is a beautiful woman without discretion."[4] The text here distinguishes Abigail from such a woman: "the woman *was* discerning and beautiful" (v.3b). The Lord didn't commission Abigail for this make-or-break mission merely because she was beautiful. He knew that she ran deep, she had discretion, she was wise, *and* she was beautiful. She was the kind of person described by the Earl of Lytton:

---

2. Gen 43:11b.

3. Gen 32:13-21. It is also of note that both Abigail and Jacob "brought up the rear," sending their servants and the presents ahead of them to appease the one they would be confronting. Jacob told his servants to tell Esau, "'Moreover, your servant Jacob is behind us.'" For he thought, 'I may appease him with the present that goes ahead of me, and afterward I shall see his face. Perhaps he will accept me.' So the present passed on ahead of him, and he himself stayed that night in the camp" (Gen 32:20-21).

4. Prov 11:22.

It is a wonderful advantage to a man, in every pursuit or avocation, to secure an adviser in a sensible woman. In woman there is at once a subtle delicacy of tact [and] plain soundness of judgment which are rarely combined to an equal degree in man. A woman, if she be really your friend, will have a sensitive regard for your character, honor, [and] repute. She will seldom counsel you to do a shabby thing; for a woman friend always desires to be proud of you.[5]

Lytton's woman is the same as that portrayed in Proverbs 31. Among other virtues, the author wrote that

Strength and dignity are her clothing,
and she laughs at the time to come.
She opens her mouth with wisdom,
and the teaching of kindness is on her tongue.[6]

ABIGAIL'S HUMILITY

David surely was attracted to Abigail's humility, evident by her mode of transport, a donkey. As mentioned previously, this is how Jesus approached Jerusalem, less than a week before his death and resurrection, specifically fulfilling Zechariah's prophecy:

Say to Daughter Zion,
"See, your king comes to you,
gentle and riding on a donkey,
and on a colt, the foal of a donkey."[7]

The similarity between Abigail and Jesus is striking. Both rode donkeys. Both carried the message of salvation, carried it meekly, and both held a strong attraction to their audience because of their evident humility.

Someone more potent than a battalion of fighting men was marching toward David. A humble, wise, strong, dignified, courageous, discerning, tactful, articulate, brilliant, beautiful, and Holy Spirit filled tsunami was about to hit David's shore. He had best be on the lookout!

---

5. Bulwer-Lytton, *AZ Quotes*, https://www.azquotes.com/ quote 1126107, accessed 5/10/2023.

6. Prov 31:25-26.

7. Zech 9:9. *See also* Matt 21:1-9; Mark 11:1-10; Luke 19:28-40; John 12:14-16.

ABIGAIL APPEARS BEFORE DAVID

David and his 400 men had already broken camp in the wilderness and were on the march, swords strapped to their thighs, headed toward Nabal's ranch (v.13b). But way off in the distance, David could make out a dark line on the horizon. It was moving. At first, he couldn't tell what it was. He pulled his troops to a halt and shaded his eyes. He now could see that it was a procession, and it appeared to be snaking its way toward him. Could this be Nabal's men on the march? Had they discovered his plan? But as the caravan came nearer, he saw that it wasn't a military posse, or at least not a very good one, because he could see that the dark line consisted of donkeys, and donkeys aren't used in battle. As they got closer, he could see that there was a woman riding astride the last donkey, and then he knew for certain that this would be peaceful, for women weren't used in battle either. The lead donkeys passed him by, and then all the rest of them. He and the woman were now face to face, and

> [w]hen Abigail saw David, she hurried and got down from the donkey and fell before David on her face and bowed to the ground. She fell at his feet and said, "On me alone, my lord, be the guilt. Please let your servant speak in your ears, and hear the words of your servant. Let not my lord regard this worthless fellow, Nabal, for as his name is, so is he. Nabal is his name, and folly is with him. But I your servant did not see the young men of my lord, whom you sent. Now then, my lord, as the LORD lives, and as your soul lives, because the LORD has restrained you from bloodguilt and from saving with your own hand, now then let your enemies and those who seek to do evil to my lord be as Nabal. And now let this present that your servant has brought to my lord be given to the young men who follow my lord. Please forgive the trespass of your servant. For the LORD will certainly make my lord a sure house, because my lord is fighting the battles of the LORD, and evil shall not be found in you so long as you live. If men rise up to pursue you and to seek your life, the life of my lord shall be bound in the bundle of the living in the care of the LORD your God. And the lives of your enemies he shall sling out as from the hollow of a sling. And when the LORD has done to my lord according to all the good that he has spoken concerning you and has appointed you prince over Israel, my lord shall have no cause of grief or pangs of conscience for having shed blood without cause or for my lord working salvation himself. And when the LORD has dealt well with my lord, then remember your servant." (vv.23-31)

A MASTERFUL SPEECH

Now that's a hefty bit of reading, but it is essential to consider the passage as a whole in order to appreciate it. It has everything to do with David's response and consequent actions. The reader should review it more than once, in part because it is a masterful piece of diplomacy, but more importantly because it was the Holy Spirit who had commissioned Abigail to go to David armed with this message.[8] What Abigail said carried with it divine authority.

We might wonder when it was that Abigail prepared this speech. Some preachers I have known say that it takes weeks to think about and compose a decent sermon. But Abigail's servant had told her about David's plan only a little bit earlier in the day. Then she had to put together a feast for an army, assemble a donkey train, load the donkeys, dress for the occasion, and make the trip. A woman's work is never done. When did she have the time to compose this declamatory *magnum opus*? The answer is, she didn't.

THE HOLY SPIRIT HELPED ABIGAIL

Though circumstantial, I believe this too is evidence of the Holy Spirit's work in Abigail. He is perfectly able to guide our lips when we are at a loss for words no matter what the circumstances, and no matter how flawed the messenger. Jesus told his disciples:

> [W]hen they bring you before the synagogues and the rulers and the authorities, do not be anxious about how you should defend yourself or what you should say, for the Holy Spirit will teach you in that very hour what you ought to say.[9]

Abigail didn't have time to prepare a studiously composed, generously footnoted lecture. It is true that she wasn't being dragged before hostile rulers and authorities as were Jesus' disciples. But like them, she was under extraordinary pressure, and humanly speaking she had every reason to believe that David would be hostile. The Holy Spirit that Jesus was talking about would "teach [her] in that very hour what [she] ought to say." So she was well fortified and well prepared.

8. "And David said to Abigail, 'Blessed be the LORD, the God of Israel, who sent you this day to meet me!'" (v.32).

9. Luke 12:11-12.

ABIGAIL SHOULDERS RESPONSIBILITY

After dismounting her donkey, Abigail fell on her face before David. As evidenced by what she said afterward, this was not feigned humility; it was not meant to "kiss up" to David. She meant it. She knew that she was bowing before royalty, because she already knew that David would take the throne. As we shall see, that is one of the primary reasons she said what she said. She wanted to protect the future king and the kingdom he would come to rule.

"On me alone, my lord, be the guilt," she begins. This opening sentence was straightforward and brilliant. Though perhaps somewhat gratuitous, she was immediately attempting to defuse David's rage by deflecting his anger away from Nabal and taking full responsibility upon herself ("on me *alone*") for any offense.

But she wasn't really doing this to protect Nabal; what Nabal gained would be but a byproduct of her plea to David. What she was doing, in addition to stemming David's anger, is introducing herself to him as the spokesperson for Nabal's household. She's saying to David, "I'm the one you can (and must) deal with, not my drunken fool husband." She takes full responsibility for what has happened and establishes her own authority in eight words when translated into English (only four in the original Hebrew). It demonstrates wisdom and superb economy of language.

PLEASE, LISTEN!

Her first request in this eloquent plea is that David would *listen* to her. She has some things of substance to say, and she doesn't want David to think she is just an upset housewife trying to get a pass for her errant husband. This will be important, David, so I need your full attention. Please, my lord, listen up!

Preachers today can learn from Abigail. Usually, we congregants need a simple reminder to *listen*. It's typical for us to come into the sanctuary with all kinds of worldly "messages" on our mind, and we now need to focus on the one message coming from the pulpit. The late great Baptist preacher Charles Stanley used this reminder for his hearers to listen often and effectively: "Now listen!" or simply "Listen!—." A drowsy congregation needs to be awakened.

Here Jesus is our best example. He repeatedly cried out "He that has ears to hear, let him hear!" The Apostle Paul did the same: "Then Paul stood up, and motioning with his hand said, 'Men of Israel, and you who fear God, listen!'"[10] And God the Father said the same to our whole race when, at the Transfiguration on the mountain, he spoke out of the cloud and said, "This is my beloved Son, with whom I am well pleased; *listen* to him."[11] It is no accident that the record of that event, commanding the attending disciples, us and mankind as a whole to listen to the Word made flesh, appears in all three of the Synoptics.[12] When Abigail asked David to "[p]lease let your servant speak in your ears, and hear the words of your servant" (v.24b) she said it only once. But she was also like the town crier, shouting three times: "Hear ye, Hear ye, Hear ye!" to all the world, because she would speak the Gospel.

I AM ABIGAIL, NOT NABAL

She immediately distances herself from her husband and isn't doing it just for effect. She honestly had no respect whatever for Nabal: "Let not my lord regard this worthless fellow, Nabal, for as his name is, so is he. Nabal is his name, and folly is with him" (v.25b). If she had been attempting to protect Nabal, or simply using him as a foil to protect the household, she would have said something like "I think my Nabe was just having a bad day yesterday. He's normally an OK guy. He often says things when he's had too much to drink that he later regrets." But she stated the truth: he's a "worthless fellow" and implies that this condition was permanent: he was always this way, drunk or sober.

Nabal may have been rich, but he had become a first-rate embarrassment to Abigail and the whole household. Abigail wanted David to know right out of the gate that the insulting message Nabal had sent him was a message from a fool, and that she had nothing to do with it; she didn't even know David had sent messengers to Nabal in the first place (v.25b). Everyone knows he is a fool, she intimates, so don't take what he says seriously or personally. He does this kind of thing all the time, he does it to everyone, and we hate it. We're always cleaning up after him.

10. Acts 13:16.

11. Matt 17:5 (emphasis added).

12. *See also* Mark 9:7 and Luke 9:35.

She then implies that if she had known what David had requested by way of food, she would have seen to it that the result would have been much different: "But I your servant did not see the young men of my lord, whom you sent." Again, she is distancing herself from Nabal and assuring David that she *of course* would have treated him decently and with respect because his was a fair request, and he deserved it. She would have answered with food, not derision.

ABIGAIL SPEAKS IN THE PAST TENSE

Abigail then makes an astonishing statement: "Now then, my lord, as the LORD lives, and as your soul lives, because the LORD has restrained you from bloodguilt and from saving with your own hand . . ." (v.26a).

Abigail here announces to David that the Lord "*has* restrained you from bloodguilt" before David had said a word. It was a *fait accompli*, an accomplished fact. She is, I believe, prophesying. The Lord had sent her on this mission; both she and David knew that instinctively (v.32). The Holy Spirit had not only sent her and guided her as she spoke but had given her foreknowledge as to certain outcomes. This is further evidenced by what she says next:

> . . . now then let your enemies and those who seek to do evil to my lord be as Nabal. (v.26b)

Abigail was not wishing upon David's enemies that they would suddenly become brutish fools firing off insulting messages, which was Nabal's present state. The clear implication is that she wants to see David's enemies *dead*,[13] just like Nabal—but Nabal was still living! Thus it would appear that the Holy Spirit had also given Abigail foreknowledge of Nabal's death (v.38). Her husband had only about ten days to live, and though she didn't state or even know when he would die, she implies that his death was also a *fait accompli*—it too was as good as done. God had revealed these facts to Abigail, and she was prophesying.

Abigail was not a prophet in the same way that Miriam, Deborah, Huldah and Anna were.[14] They apparently held the office, which Abigail

---

13. By including the words "and those who seek to do evil to my lord" Abigail, perhaps unwittingly, was wishing or predicting death for Saul, who was presently pursuing David.

14. Miriam, Ex 15:20; Deborah, Jdg 4:4; Huldah, 2 Kgs 22:14; Anna, Luke 2:36.

did not. But one did not need to hold the office in order to prophesy, that is, to deliver a prophetic word (or to prophesy in a state of ecstasy as Saul and others did).[15] David himself is called a prophet in this more restricted sense of someone who delivered a prophetic word. The Apostle Peter said, "[David] was a prophet and knew that God had promised him on oath that he would place one of his descendants on his throne."[16]

DAVID'S FUTURE IS GUARANTEED

Abigail continues, now turning her attention to what was coming for David further down the line:

> For the LORD will certainly make my lord a sure house, because my lord is fighting the battles of the LORD, and evil shall not be found in you so long as you live. If men rise up to pursue you and to seek your life, the life of my lord shall be bound in the bundle of the living in the care of the LORD your God. And the lives of your enemies he shall sling out as from the hollow of a sling. (vv.28b-29)

Abigail has now shifted to the future tense. Although it is clear from the context that she wants these things to come true for David, that is not the thrust of her message. This are not "may it be so" statements but "it will be so." David *will* have a "sure house,"[17] he *will* be "bound in the bundle of the living" and his enemies God *will* "sling out" (David, being an expert with the sling, would particularly appreciate her use of the term "sling out").

None of the promises and statements in verses 28 and 29 were matters that Abigail could have made on her own authority. She promised David that he "certainly" *will* have a sure house, that he was fighting God's battles, that sin *would* never be found in him, and that he *would* be safe from his pursuers. These promises are put forth as future facts, not as Abigail's wish list.[18] Furthermore, close to the end of her message she certified that these

15. 1 Sam 19:24.

16. Acts 2:30.

17. The "sure house" of which Abigail is speaking is described further by Isaiah: "Therefore thus says the LORD God, 'Behold, I am the one who has laid as a foundation in Zion a stone, a tested stone, a precious cornerstone, of a *sure foundation* . . .'" (Isa 55:16a) (emphasis added). *See also* Ps 122:3: "Jerusalem [is] built as a city that is bound firmly together."

18. Abigail also assumes the future outcome: "And *when* the LORD has done to my lord according to all the good that he has spoken concerning you . . ." (v.30a) (emphasis added).

promises were indeed what God had spoken: "And when the LORD has done to my lord *according to all the good that he has spoken concerning you* . . ." (v.30a) (emphasis added). Her words were from the Holy Spirit; she did not speak on her own authority. Hers were prophetic words.

DEATH FOR DAVID'S ENEMIES

In the Psalms, David often prays that the Lord will execute judgment on those who sought to destroy him. In Psalm 109, for example, he asks God to "[l]et them be before the LORD continually, that he may cut off the memory of them from the earth!"[19] This is a bold prayer, and one that human beings might be reluctant to embrace, because the future for those whom God would "sling out" holds his wrathful judgment:

> But those who seek to destroy my life
>> shall go down into the depths of the earth;
> they shall be given over to the power of the sword;
>> they shall be a portion for jackals.[20]

We do not know whether David would have specifically maintained such a wish for the destruction of Saul.[21] But he had asked the Lord to avenge him of the evil Saul had done to him.[22] And Abigail describes Saul well when she says to David: "If men *rise up to pursue you and to seek your life*, the life of my lord shall be bound in the bundle of the living in the care of the LORD your God" (v.29a) (emphasis added). Saul was in constant pursuit of David and meant to kill him. Again, Abigail is not merely saying that she hopes that this will be true for David. Rather, she is saying that when that kind of thing happens, as it is presently happening with Saul, he can be absolutely assured that his (David's) life will be "bound in the bundle of the living," that is, in the Lord's care and love. Later in life, as he looked

---

19. Ps 109:15.

20. Ps 63:9-10.

21. Whether David hoped for the immediate destruction of Saul or not, it is clear from scripture that he was not going to be the one to destroy him. After he had spared Saul's life in the cave, David told him: "May the Lord judge between me and you, may the Lord avenge me against you, but my hand shall not be against you" (1 Sam 24:12). In the imprecatory psalms David prays the same, that is, for God, not David, to bring judgment against the wicked.

22. 1 Sam 24:12.

back upon his own experiences, David would affirm that Abigail was right, and he would pass that truth along to all of us:

> The LORD watches over you—the LORD is your shade at your right hand; the sun will not harm you by day, nor the moon by night. The LORD will keep you from all harm—*he will watch over your life*; the LORD will watch over your coming and going both now and forevermore.[23]

ABIGAIL'S INNER BEAUTY

We have already seen that Abigail spoke by unction of the Holy Spirit, who was living within her. He gave her the words to speak; her message to David was in fact the Holy Spirit's. But the Holy Spirit could have used anyone or anything to deliver the message, including Abigail's donkey. He did so about 400 years earlier, when a donkey delivered a message from the Lord to the reckless false prophet Balaam.[24] The Holy Spirit could have used a rock[25] to speak to David if he had wanted to, and spared Abigail the trip.

But we can see that there is more to Abigail than her message. There is a spirit in her that draws us to her, a spirit that drew David to her too. Such a spirit does not dwell in a donkey or a rock. Abigail was a beautiful woman not only physically but spiritually. She was consonant with Peter's instruction to the women of the Gentile church:

> Your beauty should not come from outward adornment, such as elaborate hairstyles and the wearing of gold jewelry or fine clothes. Rather, it should be that of your inner self, the unfading beauty of a gentle and quiet spirit, which is of great worth in God's sight.[26]

23. Ps 121:5-8 (emphasis added).

24. Num 22:21-39. *See also* 2 Pet 2:16, where the apostle reminds us that "[Balaam] was rebuked for his own transgression; a speechless donkey spoke with human voice and restrained the prophet's madness."

25. Luke 19:40.

26. 1 Pet 3:3-4. *See also* Prov 31:30: "Charm is deceitful, and beauty is vain, but a woman who fears the Lord is to be praised."

FRUIT OF THE SPIRIT

Once people come to faith in Jesus, the Holy Spirit comes to dwell in them. When the Spirit takes up residence there, the believer begins to bear fruit. As it grows, the fruit becomes increasingly convincing evidence that something has changed in the person who has come to faith. That is the primary way in which we can tell if one *is* a believer, that he or she has a *credible* profession of faith in the Lord Jesus—that is, through evidence of the fruit of the Spirit in their life.

The Apostle Paul identifies this "fruit" for us in his letter to the Christians in Galatia:

> But the fruit of the Spirit is love, joy, peace, patience, kindness, goodness, faithfulness, gentleness, self-control; against such things there is no law.[27]

Abigail displayed this fruit. Her trip to meet with David was in itself motivated by *love*—her evident love for David, for her country Israel, and for the Lord. She doesn't seem bubbly, but she is *joyful*. She could have come with tears rolling down her cheeks, considering the imminent slaughter that awaited her household. Her spirits were lifted, of course, buoyed by her early knowledge[28] that David would receive her message with joy and thanksgiving.[29] But she came to David when the immediate future looked very bleak to her. Thus, we can see that her joy did not come from her present situation, but from the One who dwelled in her.

ABIGAIL DISPLAYED PEACE

Of course, Abigail's most immediate and urgent concern was to bring *peace*. We will discuss this further in chapter 8, but suffice it here for us to observe how she brought peace, and what kind of peace she brought. She carried it to David and his camp in that they were turned back from battling with Nabal. She brought it to her hometown Carmel by delivering its citizens from the sirens of war and brutal bloodshed. She brought it to

27. Gal 5:22–23.

28. Abigail knew before David responded to her that the Holy Spirit had worked in him to bring agreement, because, as mentioned previously, she spoke as though her request had already been granted.

29. "And David said to Abigail, 'Blessed be the LORD, the God of Israel, who sent you this day to meet me!'" (v.32).

Nabal's servants because David had planned to kill them all. She brought internal peace to David, both from keeping him from shedding innocent blood and from having to be burdened with a resultant guilty conscience for the rest of his life. Abigail was a *peace*maker.

The immediate peace that Abigail was able to bring in delivering others from a bloody conflict is something that human beings can bring about. Peace-loving nations often send "peacekeeping missions" to places in the world where there is no peace but war or threatened war, and they very often are successful in their mission. For example, Jimmy Carter was successful in doing so in the Middle East during his term as president. But no human peacekeeping mission can bring the "peace of God, which surpasses all understanding,"[30] a peace that Jesus said is a commodity that the world simply does not possess, and therefore cannot give.[31] Abigail could not bring that kind of peace on her own, but she was able to bring it because she was empowered by the Holy Spirit. Because she turned David away from his plans, she brought inner peace—Holy Ghost peace—to the man who would someday reign over Israel.

ABIGAIL DISPLAYED ALL THE FRUIT OF THE SPIRIT

By her gracious and appealing demeanor, Abigail also displayed *patience, kindness, goodness, gentleness* and *self-control*.[32] She made no demands of David. She desperately needed an immediate answer but showed *patience* in not insisting. Abigail knew that "[w]ith patience a ruler may be persuaded, and the soft tongue will break a bone."[33] She was remarkably *gentle* in her approach.[34] She exhibited *self-control*. This was an emergency, a life

---

30. Phil 4:7.

31. John 14:27.

32. Abigail's character and demeanor were also consonant with what Paul wrote to the church in Colossae: "So, as those who have been chosen of God, holy and beloved, put on a heart of compassion, kindness, humility, gentleness, and patience" (Col 3:12).

33. Prov 24:15.

34. Abigail exhibited gentleness (translated "meekness," KJV) when "she fell before David on her face and bowed to the ground," when she referred to herself as David's "servant" and "my lord," and when she asked David to "[p]lease forgive the trespass of your servant . . ." She also showed gentleness by arriving on a donkey, just as Jesus did on Palm Sunday: "Say to the daughter of Zion, 'See, your king comes to you, *gentle* and riding on a donkey, and on a colt, the foal of a donkey'" (Matt 21:5, NIV) (emphasis added). *See also* Zech 9:9.

and death matter, and one might have expected her to have been outraged beyond control, or overcome with emotion, frantic, or all the above. But if she had such tendencies, she was able to overcome them by being able, as Rudyard Kipling said, to "keep your head when all about you are losing theirs." "Keeping your head" is possible in an extraordinary, supernatural way for those who have the Holy Spirit, for "God hath not given us the spirit of fear; but of power, and of love, and of a *sound mind*."[35]

Above all else, Abigail showed *faithfulness*. Though she may not have wished any favors for her husband Nabal, she was nevertheless being faithful to him and especially to his servants, whose lives were at stake. She was being faithful to David—not the temporarily "mad" David, but the clear-minded, anointed David. And recognizing that he was already the anointed king of Israel, she was being faithful to the country and its citizenry, protecting their future king from jeopardizing his reputation, thereby weakening righteousness and justice in the realm.

BEING A FAITHFUL STEWARD IS RISKY BUSINESS

But the most poignant aspect of Abigail's faithfulness was her unflinching adherence to the Holy Spirit's message, to tell David exactly what God had told her to say. She exhibited a kind of apostolic stewardship. Like Paul, she knew that she had been entrusted with the Word of God and was duty-bound to execute her stewardship faithfully. Paul told the Thessalonians that "just as we have been approved by God to be entrusted with the gospel, so we speak, not to please man, but to please God who tests our hearts."[36]

Surely it was not easy for Abigail to carry out her mission. As we will examine further in chapter 8, in speaking God's word she had to be invasive, and could not have been sure what David's reaction would be. She endangered herself, just as Nathan risked his life when he rebuked King David for stealing Bathsheba and murdering Uriah. She was also like Esther, who risked her life before King Ahasuerus when she approached him to plead for the Jews. Esther well knew that the king might reject her, which would mean the death sentence, but said: "I will go to the king, though it is against the law, and if I perish, I perish."[37]

35. 2 Tim 1:7, KJV (emphasis added).
36. 1 Thess 2:4.
37. Esth 4:16b.

We now know the "rest of the story" for Esther, Nathan and Abigail. In each case, God chose to spare them. But we should not forget the "in between" segment, the gap between when they determined in their hearts to be faithful to the Lord's command and the time when the verdict was made known, that is, when they learned whether they would live or die. Other examples can be found where the outcome was not so happy, like John the Baptist who rebuked Herod for immorality and was beheaded,[38] or Stephen, who faithfully proclaimed God's word to the Jews and was stoned to death.[39] There is real risk in being faithful, and Abigail passed the test.

ABIGAIL'S PROPHESIES WOULD BE FULFILLED

Abigail's prophesies all came true, one of the biblical requirements for true prophecy.[40] Close to the end of his life, just before David commissioned his son Solomon to build the temple, David testified to that fact, as he had witnessed it in his life:

> Then King David went in and sat before the LORD and said, "Who am I, O LORD God, and what is my house, that you have brought me thus far? And yet this was a small thing in your eyes, O LORD God. You have spoken also of your servant's house for a great while to come, and this is instruction for mankind, O LORD God! And what more can David say to you? For you know your servant, O LORD God! Because of your promise, and according to your own heart, you have brought about all this greatness, to make your servant know it.[41]

ABIGAIL WAS ASSURED OF THE OUTCOME

A reading of Abigail's entire speech reveals something else. Not once does she make an outright demand that David change his plans. Abigail had apparently developed an art that some lawyers have: to argue their client's case

38. Mark 6:14-29.

39. Acts 7:54-60.

40. "[W]hen a prophet speaks in the name of the LORD, if the word does not come to pass or come true, that is a word that the LORD has not spoken; the prophet has spoken it presumptuously. You need not be afraid of him" (Deut 18:22).

41. 2 Sam 7:18-21.

in such a way that the judge or jury will come up with the desired judgment or verdict on their own, or at least think they did.

For example, in a jury trial the attorney will present the case in such a way that the issue becomes a question that needs to be answered by the jurors using their own reasoning, rather than simply adopting predictable conclusions that the lawyer otherwise might have urged them to adopt. The attorney never tells the jury or judge precisely what she wants them to do. She simply proves up and argues the facts of the case and lets the jury figure it out on their own. Abigail, by not making a direct plea for cancelation of David's plan, is doing the same thing. Like a good lawyer, she wanted David to think this through for himself, because he would then own the decision as his verdict, not merely the adoption of hers.

But Abigail wasn't merely using the art of good argument. She didn't have to make an express petition because she already had assurance that God had changed, or was in the process of changing, David's heart. God had sovereignly guaranteed the outcome, evidenced by what Abigail said at the outset, before David told her that he had changed his plans. The verdict was already in, though David would not announce it until verse 35.[42]

ABIGAIL'S MESSAGE WAS PIVOTAL

That is not to say, however, that Abigail's visit wasn't necessary. It was pivotal. None of this would have happened without her. She was reciting and confirming for David what God had done, is doing, and will do. He was in dire need of her message. He needed to be reminded that God was sovereign, that he was in complete control. And God was working in Abigail's audience of one; he softened David's heart and made him receptive to her counsel. The Holy Spirit's work in both of them is unmistakable, as we shall further see from David's response.

QUESTIONS FOR THOUGHT

1. What were Abigail's motivations for intervening on behalf of Nabal? Was her primary goal to protect her husband? What greater motivations are evident?

---

42. There, David said: "See, I have obeyed your voice, and I have granted your petition."

2. Abigail demonstrated the fruit of the Spirit. How did this help her in communicating with David, and in turning him away from his plan to kill Nabal? Do you know people like Abigail, who show the fruit of the Spirit in the way in which they communicate? Do you act in this way?

3. Do you take risks in communicating the Word of God to others? Do the risks sometimes hold you back from witnessing? What can help the Christian to speak forthrightly, not fearing the consequences? Is it a matter of priorities?

5. DAVID

We can see that Abigail's message was pivotal to the outcome in part because David so testified. David said that Abigail's visit caused him to change his mind: "And David said to Abigail, 'Blessed be the LORD, the God of Israel, who sent you this day to meet me! Blessed be your discretion, and blessed be you, who have kept me this day from bloodguilt and from working salvation with my own hand! For as surely as the LORD, the God of Israel, lives, who has restrained me from hurting you, *unless you had hurried and come to meet me*, truly by morning there had not been left to Nabal so much as one male'" (vv.32–34) (emphasis added).

FROM ETERNITY PAST

This may seem baffling. We have seen that Abigail could state to David that God had *already* "restrained you from bloodguilt" (v.26) before she came to visit, yet David states here that "as surely as the LORD, the God of Israel, lives" if she hadn't "hurried and come to meet [him]," he would have carried through with his nefarious plan. Did Abigail's visit change things, or was it foreordained? The Westminster Confession of Faith says *both* are true simultaneously:

> God, from all eternity, did, by the most wise and holy counsel of His own will, freely, and unchangeably ordain whatsoever comes to pass, yet so, as thereby neither is God the author of sin, *nor is violence offered to the will of the creatures*; nor is the liberty or contingency of second causes taken away, but rather established.[1]

---

1. *Westminster Confession & Catechism*, 3.1, 23 (emphasis added). *See also* Rayburn,

The feeble human mind cannot fully comprehend such truths. Abigail chose to visit, and her visit made the difference. Yet both her choice and that difference had been foreordained. John Calvin, in his *Institutes of the Christian Religion*, said that it is best for us to understand those two truths, and then leave the matter alone.[2] David himself wrote that "my eyes are not raised too high; I do not occupy myself with things too great and too marvelous for me."[3] David rightly attributes to Abigail her wise choice to come quickly and advise him, yet all the while both he and Abigail recognize that it was the LORD who sent her in the first place (v.32) and prepared David's heart to respond as he did—though, like Calvin, they couldn't piece it all together!

Abigail and David were both speaking and acting within God's sovereign plan, and they seem to have sensed it. That is not always so with believers. Very often God takes us through experiences in which, at the time, we are utterly blind as to his sovereign plan; he often keeps us from seeing it until later (if he discloses it at all). But here both parties were cognizant of the fact that God had arranged the whole thing, all the while understanding that their words and actions were truly *their* words freely spoken and actions freely done, crucial to the outcome.

DAVID'S APPRECIATION OF GOD'S SOVEREIGN LOVE FOR HIM

We too often forget what David here remembered. Abigail had brought him to his senses, out of a tantrum. When he realized that, his first order of business was to *thank God* for bringing him to his senses: "Blessed be the LORD, the God of Israel, who sent you this day to meet me!" (v.32).

The Truth, 95: "If destiny is writ large in Holy Scripture, so is contingency."

2. John Calvin, in setting out the limits of human beings to fully comprehend predestination, wrote: "[L]et them remember that when they inquire into predestination, they are penetrating the sacred precincts of divine wisdom. If anyone with carefree assurance breaks into this place, he will not succeed in satisfying his curiosity and he will enter a labyrinth from which he can find no exit. For it is not right for man unrestrainedly to search out things that the Lord has willed to be hid in himself, and to unfold from eternity itself the [most sublime] wisdom, which he would have us revere but not understand that through this also he should fill us with wonder. He has set forth by his Word the secrets of his will that he has decided to reveal to us. These he decided to reveal in so far as he foresaw that they would concern us and benefit us." Calvin, *Institutes*, 3.21.1, 922-923.

3. Ps 131:1.

Then he thanked Abigail: "Blessed be your discretion, and blessed be you, who have kept me this day from bloodguilt and from working salvation with my own hand!" (v.33).

This is typical of David. When the Lord sent Nathan to David to condemn his sin against Uriah,[4] David's first response was "I have sinned against the LORD."[5] One might have thought that he would first say "I have sinned against Uriah," which of course he had. To human beings, that was his clear and most obvious sin. But all sin is first and foremost against God, and David knew that well. While he was in the depths of despair regarding his sin against Uriah, David narrowed it even further when he said that he had sinned *only* against the Lord:

> For I know my transgressions,
> and my sin is ever before me.
> *Against you, you only, have I sinned*
> and done what is evil in your sight,
> so that you may be justified in your words
> and blameless in your judgment.[6]

In blessing, David's first response was to the Lord. In sin, David's first repair was to the Lord. Though we receive blessings from others or sin against others, our essential relationship is with God alone, for it is in him that "we live and move and have our being."[7] That is why David in this instance with Abigail first blessed the Lord.

NO EXCUSES

In David's response to Nathan we can see one of the reasons God told Samuel that he was choosing him over others as Israel's future king. David's heart was right before God, and that was what God was most concerned about.[8] God saw something in David's heart that pleased him, and we can see it as well. David sinned, but he didn't make excuses for having sinned; he admitted it before he could scrounge up an excuse. This is in

4. 2 Sam 12:1-13.

5. 2 Sam 12:13.

6. Ps 51:3-4 (emphasis added).

7. Acts 17:28a.

8. "For the LORD sees not as man sees: man looks on the outward appearance, but the LORD looks on the heart" (1 Sam 16:7b).

stark contrast to David's predecessor. When Saul was confronted by Samuel who rebuked him for his disobedience to God's command to utterly destroy the Amalekites and everything they had, Saul first lied, claiming that he had destroyed everything, and then (without admitting to his lie)[9] started to make excuses, blaming others:

> And Samuel came to Saul, and Saul said to him, "Blessed be you to the LORD. I have performed the commandment of the LORD." And Samuel said, "What then is this bleating of the sheep in my ears and the lowing of the oxen that I hear?" Saul said, "They have brought them from the Amalekites, for the people spared the best of the sheep and of the oxen to sacrifice to the LORD your God, and the rest we have devoted to destruction." Then Samuel said to Saul, "Stop!"[10]

Stop! Stop making excuses! Stop blaming others! Just "man up," Saul, like your successor David would. God doesn't want excuses; he wants repentance.

DAVID WAS A LISTENER

Much can be learned about David from verses 32–34. First, in the main, David was a *listener*. He listened to the prophet Nathan. He listened to a widow from Tekoa, and thus listened to Joab urging David to reconcile with his son Absalom.[11] He was a commander who listened to his men.[12] He listened to Joab, commander of Israel's troops, when Joab rebuked David for mourning excessively for Absalom, when Absalom's life had been taken

9. Satan did essentially the same when he appeared before God the second time in the book of Job. Having been proven wrong, claiming that Job would curse God if Job lost all his property and children, Satan did not have the integrity to admit that he had been wrong when Job responded to the loss by saying "The LORD gave, and the LORD has taken away; blessed be the name of the LORD" (Job 1:21b). Satan and Saul both ignored the obvious truth, and continued their conversations without missing a beat.

10. 1 Sam 15:13–16a (emphasis added).

11. 2 Sam 14:1–22. "Then the woman said, 'Please let your servant speak a word to my lord the king.' He said, 'Speak'" (v.12).

12. "But David's men said to him, 'Behold, we are afraid here in Judah; how much more then if we go to Keilah against the armies of the Philistines?' *Then David inquired of the Lord again.* And the Lord answered him, 'Arise, go down to Keilah, for I will give the Philistines into your hand'" (1 Sam 23:3–4) (emphasis added). *See also* 1 Chr 13:1–4, where David first asked "all the assembly of Israel" for their consent, and then waited for it, before being willing to bear the Ark of the Covenant to Jerusalem.

for his attempted coup.[13] Most significantly, he inquired of the Lord before making military decisions (this case being an exception), and then listened to and obeyed the Lord's counsel. David was like Isaiah in this way:

> Morning by morning he awakens;
> he awakens my ear
> to hear as those who are taught.
> The LORD God has opened my ear
> to hear as those who are taught.
> The LORD God has opened my ear
> and I was not rebellious;
> I turned not backward.[14]

Abigail wasn't accustomed to a man who listened to her, at least not when the man happened to be her husband. Nabal's own servant said that "he is such a worthless man that one cannot speak to him" (v.17b). And when Abigail first learned of David's plans, she didn't even bother to approach her husband because she knew it would be a waste of time; he wouldn't listen anyway. Yet she felt that she could approach David, and that he might listen—notwithstanding his plan to Pearl Harbor all of Nabalville.

David's response was instant and positive because he did indeed listen to Abigail. He believed in the need to listen to wise counsel, and apparently taught this principle to his son Solomon, who later wrote that "a wise man will hear and increase in learning, and a man of understanding will acquire wise counsel."[15] When he listened to Abigail, he discovered that what she said resonated with who he was, who he wanted to be, and with what the Lord had already taught him. Abigail wasn't telling David anything that he hadn't heard before. He knew instantly that she was right.

DON'T EVEN THIINK ABOUT IT

David answered Abigail as soon as the words were out of her mouth. He knew that he, like everyone, had the propensity to roll things over in his mind before answering someone who had rebuked or challenged him. There are many examples in scripture of how a believer should react, and others showing how not to react. We will look at one of each.

13. 2 Sam 9:1-8.
14. Isa 50:4-5.
15. Prov 1:5.

Daniel 3 records the story of Shadrach, Meshach, and Abednego, who refused to bow down to Nebuchadnezzar. When Nebuchadnezzar got word of their obstinance, he was magnanimous enough to give them a second chance, but warned them that if they persisted, he would have them thrown into a "burning, fiery furnace." The three responded that "we are not *careful* to answer thee in this matter,"[16] and thus were thrown into the inferno. When they said "we are not careful" they didn't mean that they were being care*less*. They meant that they had already thought the matter over, knew beforehand what their answer would be, and would not roll it over in their minds again. They knew that to do so would be dangerous. Thus they gave an immediate answer, just as David had done when Nathan rebuked him. These three Jewish heroes and David knew the truth already and were not going to rethink things.

GEHAZI SINNED WHEN HE MULLED IT OVER

There is great danger in "rethinking" what you already know, as demonstrated by Gehazi, Elisha's servant. The story is recorded in Second Kings 5. Elisha had just healed the Syrian General Naaman. Naaman, overjoyed, wanted to pay for services rendered, but Elisha emphatically refused, even when Naaman pressed him. Elisha refused instantly and twice, invoking God's name in his refusal. He did not want Naaman to leave his premises believing that the Gospel was something a man could buy. Elisha knew his own weakness—that, being himself subject to temptation and sin,[17] it was dangerous ground for him to reconsider. But his servant Gehazi was listening in and began to roll his evil impulses over in his head. The Bible tells us of his ruminations:

> Gehazi, the servant of Elisha the man of God, *said to himself*, "My master was too easy on Naaman, this Aramean, by not accepting from him what he brought. As surely as the LORD lives, I will run after him and get something from him."[18]

16. Dan 3:16b, KJV.

17. Jesus himself is like Elisha (and us) in this respect: "For we do not have a high priest who is unable to sympathize with our weaknesses, but one who in every respect has been tempted as we are, yet without sin" (Heb 4:15).

18. 2 Kgs 5:20, NIV (emphasis added).

Gehazi, unlike the Jewish trio before Nebuchadnezzar, was "careful." Too careful. He felt he should think it over, mainly because there was so much money involved. He chased Naaman down as he was on the road back to Syria and trimmed him for two heavy bags of silver coins, about seventy-five pounds each. His reconsideration got him some big money—more than $50,000 on today's precious metals market—but with a devastating result: it doomed him to leprosy for the rest of his earthly life.[19]

David did not mull Abigail's counsel over in his brain. He was able to agree with Abigail instantly because he knew the truth already and reso-nated with her message. He recognized the danger of thinking it over. They heard the same voice and David was quick to concur with what she said.

RESONANCE

My high school science teacher once demonstrated resonance using the school's piano. He showed us that by holding down on Middle C, for ex-ample, and then striking Lower C, he could let up on Lower C and Middle C would "sing" as he continued to hold it down, though it hadn't been struck. Middle C had picked up on Lower C's frequency, which is half that of Middle C. Try it. The two frequencies are directly related. The two are friends, and one will sing when it hears the other (this works with any two keys that are an octave apart).

Abigail's words to David had such an effect on him. The two were, so to speak, on the same frequency, and though they had not previously met, they were friends already. Abigail was wife to a man who was clearly not on her frequency; it's an understatement to say that the two were discor-dant. But though this was the first time David had met Abigail, he instantly picked up on what she was saying, and she somehow knew that he would. This was because they both were under the influence of the same Holy Spirit, had read the same Bible, and like all believers, were *one* in the Spirit; that is, they were one in Christ.[20] David's heart sang like Middle C when he

19. 2 Kgs 5:27.

20. "For just as the body is one and has many members, and all the members of the body, though many, are one body, so it is with Christ. For in one Spirit we were all baptized into one body—Jews or Greeks, slaves or free—and all were made to drink of one Spirit" (1 Cor 12:12-13).

heard Abigail speak God's Word because he recognized the Voice that was speaking through her.[21] They were friends.

BELIEVERS RESONATE WITH BELIEVERS

Perhaps you have experienced the same phenomenon when you met another Christian for the first time. There is immediate rapport between the two of you. It can seem closer than earthly family ties, and that is because it *is* closer. A brother or sister in Christ is a brother or sister forever; earthly ties will end.

I have written elsewhere of an experience my daughter and I had many years ago, when we went on a short-term mission trip to Ukraine. We arrived at the Donetsk airport very late on a Saturday night. Having flown from St. Louis on four separate flights, we were glad to see our beds. But that respite was short, because early Sunday morning our hosts awakened us and took us to their Ukrainian Baptist Church. At once we found ourselves surrounded by Russian-speaking Ukrainian Christians, and with the help of whispering interpreters we were privileged to worship with them.

I had never experienced anything quite like it, nor anything more joyful. Looking about at these economically distressed Christians while joining them in their lusty singing of old Russian hymns (as well as some Western contemporary gospel, translated into Russian) brought tears to my eyes, as we recognized that only a few years earlier they had lived behind the Iron Curtain and were considered our enemies. But there was immediate joyful affinity in Christ—it was unmistakable and thrilling.

This affinity transcended all human boundaries. It was evident that God, at that very moment, was doing what he said he would do in Paul's letter to the church at Ephesus: "[f]or he himself is our peace, who has made the two groups one and has destroyed the barrier, the dividing wall of hostility."[22] Through the work of the Holy Spirit we were able to experience that verse in real time. The same Holy Spirit working in our hometown St. Louis on that sabbath day was working in Donetsk, halfway around the globe, and we were privileged to get in on it. We resonated. Like Middle C and Low C, we were friends.

Christians also resonate with the Bible when they hear it read or taught. One doesn't need to travel to another continent to experience this.

21. "My sheep hear my voice, and I know them, and they follow me" (John 10:27).
22. Eph 2:14.

Believers experience it regularly when they hear the Word of God proclaimed. It may be during a sermon, a hymn, a counseling session, or any time someone is declaring God's truth in our ears. Very often the truths that we are presently hearing resonate with truths that we already knew. So it was with David as he listened to Abigail.

JESUS RESONATED WITH UNBELIEVERS, TOO

Abigail's use of resonance was aimed at a believer, and the two found resonance in God's word which they both believed. Jesus did the same with his disciples. But he also used it regularly with unbelievers, who did not yet believe the word of God. Virtually all his parables employed the principle of resonance. Take this one, for example:

> Which of you, if your son asks for bread, will give him a stone? Or if he asks for a fish, will give him a snake? If you, then, though you are evil, know how to give good gifts to your children, how much more will your Father in heaven give good gifts to those who ask him![23]

Here, as in most of his parables, Jesus is seeking a common denominator—a harmonious chord—with the hearer. "Every one of you knows," he says, "that if your own son asks you for some bread, you're not going to give him something like a stone. You're going to give him something good to eat." The hearers resonated with that. "Of course I wouldn't give him a stone. I would give him what he asked for, because I'm his father and I love my boy." Knowing he has struck a harmonious chord, Jesus continues: "If you, then, though you are evil, know how to give good gifts to your children, how much more will your Father in heaven give good gifts to those who ask him!"

DAVID'S HUMILITY OPENED HIS EARS

David, as discussed previously,[24] was a humble man (departing from that for a few hours after getting Nabal's memo). Humility was something learned through his difficult upbringing, and early became imbedded in his character. His humility made it so that he could listen to Abigail

23. Matt 7:9–11.
24. See subhead "God Humbled David" *et seq.* in chapter 1.

when, before getting to the substance of her message, she pled with him to "[p]lease let your servant speak in your ears, and hear the words of your servant" (v.24b).

Surely it was not easy, particularly in front of his troops, for David to listen and then cave in to a housewife convincing him to countermand his own orders. But listening to her was possible because he had been humbled in the past, going all the way back to his father Jesse's farm. The Lord had prepared David for this moment, a moment of truth. We could say that Abigail had a relatively "easy target" in David, because he was not only a believer, but a humble believer.

Once again, compare David to Saul. Saul was not prepared for such a moment. As mentioned, one must be humble to listen, and Saul was by no means a humble man. When Samuel commanded Saul to wait for him to preside over the pre-battle sacrifice, Saul surely *heard* what the prophet said but we know he wasn't *listening* because he disobeyed. As a result of his being unable to listen, the kingdom was stripped from him.[25]

"WAIT, I SAY, ON THE LORD"

David was listening carefully to Abigail when she said, "Now then, my lord, as the LORD lives, and as your soul lives, because the LORD has restrained you from bloodguilt . . ." (v.26a). David, of course, did not want to be burdened with a history of bloodguilt. He knew that Saul was in fact so burdened[26] because his slaughter of the priests of Nob showed up on his criminal record.[27] As discussed in chapter 2, David had learned from Saul, though in the negative: do not do what Saul did.

One of the fundamental ways in which Saul failed was impatience. When the Lord's prophet tells you to wait for him to make a sacrifice to God, you'd best heed his command no matter what circumstances might develop. His rushing things was a lack of faith, and "without faith it is

---

25. "And Samuel said [to Saul], 'Has the LORD as great delight in burnt offerings and sacrifices, as in obeying the voice of the LORD? Behold, to obey is better than sacrifice, and to listen than the fat of rams. For rebellion is like the sin of divination, and arrogance like the evil of idolatry. Because you have rejected the word of the LORD, he has rejected you as king'" (1 Sam 15:22–23).

26. 1 Sam 22:20–23.

27. 1 Sam 22:11–19.

impossible to please God."[28] It is faith, not sacrifice, that pleases God.[29] As we have noticed, Saul *couldn't wait it out*. He had to rush things along in his own way, and thus forfeited the blessing that could have been his.[30] David surely learned from this as well. He later wrote:

> Wait on the LORD;
>> be of good courage, and he shall strengthen
>>> thine heart:
>> wait, I say, on the LORD.[31]

But in the Nabal incident, David had exited the door of God's waiting room. He was going to kill Nabal and all his men before sunup. If he had done so, he, like Saul, would have forfeited a blessing that could have been his. He had forgotten his Bible reading for the moment. He had forgotten about Abraham, the man of faith, and Abigail had to remind him to "wait on the Lord," just as David's ancestor Abraham had done.

QUESTIONS FOR THOUGHT

1. Have you experienced "resonance" with other Christians as you talk or worship together? Have you found that you resonated with the Word of God when you have heard it preached or taught? Does this help confirm your confidence as a Christian?

2. Though it's a good trait to think things over, when might it become a bad trait? Have you ever thought things over too long, and now wish that you had simply done the right thing to begin with? Why was it that you mulled it over? What motivated you?

3. Many people are like Nabal: they don't listen to others. How can you get someone to listen? Why was David able to listen when Abigail spoke to him?

28. Heb 11:6a, NIV.

29. 1 Sam 15:22.

30. Jonah 2:8b.

31. Ps 27:14, KJV. *See also* Lam 3:25-26: "The Lord is good to those who wait for him, / to the soul who seeks him / It is a good thing that one should wait quietly / for the salvation of the Lord."

6. WAITING

D avid knew his Bible well, and when he wasn't reading it, he was thinking about it. He would write "O how I love your law! It is my meditation all the day."[1] It was his intimate acquaintance with the Hebrew bible
that made Abigail's short message so effective, drawing an immediate and
positive response from David.

REMEMBERING A PATRIARCH

He already knew from reading the book of Genesis about some of his predecessors, including his many-times great grandfather Abraham.[2] Abigail
was telling David that he should simply wait on the Lord. He knew he
should, as he had formerly expressed by his refusal to kill Saul in the cave.
He knew, as she spoke, that Abigail was right. It resonated with him. But
while waiting on the Lord is the right and most fruitful thing to do, human
beings find it terribly difficult to "sit around" and wait for God to act. Even
Abraham, scripture's great exemplar of faith, found it almost impossible.[3]
But often, particularly for Christians, "sitting around" is the right thing to
do because it isn't sitting around at all—it just looks like it.

1. Ps 119:97.

2. In the Psalms, David mentions Abraham four times: once in Ps 47:9, and three
more times in Ps 105.

3. Rom 4:1–25; Gal 3:6–18; Heb 11:8–12.

ABRAHAM SAT IT OUT

David could have, and should have, drawn from the example of Abraham before mustering his troops in the Wilderness of Paon. Many of David's predecessors had learned important lessons in the wilderness. For example, Abraham, Jacob, Moses, and the nation of Israel as a whole (sadly, one segment of their education lasted forty years because of their unbelief) all learned divine truths in the wilderness. And in the New Testament, John the Baptist and Jesus himself repaired to the wilderness not merely to avoid the hubbub of the civilized world, but to learn and to pray. The Lord often uses "aloneness" as a means for communicating his perspective on life. The most important lesson David could learn from Abraham in this instance was to "Be still, and know that I am God."[4] David did indeed learn what sustained Abraham, for it would be David the Psalmist who would later write those words.

At the beginning of the covid pandemic, federal and state governments issued guidelines intended to stem the spread of the virus, including staying at home. That meant that like millions of others I personally sat a whole lot more than usual. And it was frustrating, knowing that there was a war going on out there. Doctors, nurses, and paramedics were square in the middle of it, risking their lives, but I had to stay home. The experts said that I could best help beat this pandemic by just sitting, and in that way be a key player. I had a crucial role to play. Perhaps they could have paraphrased John Milton's famous quote: "They also serve who only *sit* and wait."

The word "sitting" can indicate indifference, laziness or indolence. In such contexts it is negative—I am doing nothing when I should be doing something. But within the covid context, it was the reverse. I was doing something by doing nothing. Sitting may be right, or sitting may be wrong. It depends on the context. It depends on the who, what, why, where and when of the sitting.

IN THE HEAT OF THE DAY

Genesis 18 is a story about a man, Abraham, who was sitting: "And the LORD appeared to Abraham by the Oaks of Mamre, as he sat at the door of his tent in the heat of the day."[5] It sounds like it was in the summertime, probably

4. Ps 46:10.
5. Gen 18:1.

midday or after. I picture it as one of those hot, humid July days we experience where I live, St. Louis. I remember the late Jack Buck calling some of those suffocating afternoon Cardinals games, and when the Cards hadn't scored any runs and the game would be in the eighth inning or so, he'd often quote an old country song: "Well, there ain't nuthin' shakin' but the leaves on the trees. And they wouldn't be a-shakin' if it wasn't for the breeze." Abraham was just sitting there. Nothing happening. Maybe the Oaks of Mamre's leaves were shaking, but otherwise it was dead still.

LATE INNINGS

And it was, so to speak, late innings. It had been a quarter century since he had pulled up stakes in Ur, his hometown, about a thousand miles away. He had moved to Canaan's wilderness because the Lord had told him to, promising him that it would be here that "I will make of you a great nation, and I will bless you and make your name great, so that you will be a blessing. In you all the families of the earth will be blessed."[6] God had also promised him that he and his wife Sarah would have a son, and by that means God would make him into a great nation, even a "multitude" of nations.[7] And the Lord had been very specific about the child: he would be born to Sarah, not to another woman, and he was to be named "Isaac."[8]

Abraham was 75 years old when he had left Ur; he was now closing in on 100. For twenty-four years he had lived in a tent, wandering[9] about in an unfamiliar land.[10] He had no permanent home. He had become a nomad, a Bedouin. Nothing that the Lord had promised him in Ur or in four appearances to Abraham since that time[11] had come true. Most disappointing was the fact that Sarah had never become pregnant, and now she was past child-bearing years.[12] As Abraham sat at the door of his tent on that hot day, things looked pretty grim. Nuthin' shakin.' *Yet there he sat.*

6. Gen 12:1–3.

7. Gen 17:4.

8. Gen 17:19.

9. "They went about in skins of sheep and goats, destitute, afflicted, mistreated—of whom the world was not worthy—wandering about in deserts and mountains, and in dens and caves of the earth" (Heb 11:37–38).

10. Heb 11:9.

11. Gen 12:7, 13:14ff, 15:1ff, and 17:1ff.

12. Heb 11:11.

DOUBTS ALONG THE WAY

Abraham had entertained some serious doubts along the way. He had laughed at the prospect of Sarah's becoming pregnant at age 90.[13] He had thought he might be killed in Egypt before any of the promises were fulfilled and thus lied to protect himself;[14] he had proposed that Eliezer of Damascus might be considered his heir rather than his own son;[15] he had substituted Hagar for Sarah in order to manufacture the heir.[16] In these ways he was trying to nudge the promise along toward fulfillment, but his machinations hadn't worked. Instead, the Egypt lie had brought trouble both to Pharaoh and to Abraham's own household. The Hagar pregnancy had produced domestic strife. Apparently anything he could do wasn't going to make a difference. The ball was in God's court now, and actually always had been. He recognized that. *So there he sat.*

Abraham could have given up. He could have pulled up stakes once again—this time literally—and returned to Ur, his hometown.[17] But if he ever entertained that thought, he must have dismissed it because he never acted on it. *He stayed put.*

The Apostle Paul said that Abraham did not waver in his faith, thus obtaining righteousness before God.[18] True enough, he had lied in Egypt to save his skin, he suggested that Eliezer would make a suitable heir, he invented his own heir by fathering Ishmael, he laughed at the thought of Sarah's pregnancy. But *he did not leave.* He hung in there. Almost 100 years old, and he's still there, sitting by the door of his tent in the heat of the day. Waiting for God to do what God had promised to do.

13. Gen 17:17.

14. Gen 12:12.

15. Gen 15:2.

16. Gen 16.

17. "If they had been thinking of that land from which they had gone out, they would have had opportunity to return. But as it is, they desire a better country, that is, a heavenly one. Therefore God is not ashamed to be called their God, for he has prepared for them a city" (Heb 11:15-16).

18. "[Abraham] did not weaken in faith when he considered his own body, which was as good as dead (since he was about a hundred years old), or when he considered the barrenness of Sarah's womb. No unbelief made him waver concerning the promise of God . . ." (Rom 4:19-20a).

SITTING EXPECTANTLY

Sitting, of course, is not always the right posture. When God told Abraham to leave Ur and move to Canaan, it would have been wrong to sit. Nor is mere "sitting" of value. A right sitting occurs when you come to the end of your ideas and resources, or when year after year goes by and you don't see your prayers being answered, but you nevertheless have that basic confidence that God is on the throne and that he will not let you down. It's a resting, a repose, a time for contemplating once again what his great promises are, a time for giving glory to God simply because you know that he will keep his word. It can actually be transformed into a time of joy.

Abraham was sitting there that day *expectantly*. Not necessarily that he thought something big was going to happen on that particular day, but that at some point, that big thing would happen. That's why he stuck around, in a manner of speaking, to see how the whole thing would play out. He wanted to be there for the bottom of the ninth. He knew things would play out. God would see to that, and when the moment came, Abraham wanted to be ready for it. I believe that's why the author tells us that when Abraham saw the Three Visitors approaching his tent that day, he "ran from the tent door to meet them."[19] Ninety-nine years old, but he could still run, and was he excited! He had a pretty good idea as to what this was about, and Who it was that was coming to his tent.[20] This is what he had been *expecting*.

Whenever a believer is called upon to sit, he should sit like he sat. It doesn't have to be down time. It can be, as Abraham's was, a time for growing strong in faith, a time for once again searching out the Word of God to take hold of the fact that God is able to do, and will do, what he has promised.

ABIGAIL TAUGHT THE FAITH OF ABRAHAM

She didn't mention the patriarch, but it was the faith of Abraham that Abigail was in fact enunciating to David. David needed to do what Abraham was doing at the door of his tent. Sit down. Exercise your faith by just being still, knowing that I am God.[21] Wait. Call off your men. Relax. God has

19. Gen. 18:2.

20. "[Abraham] said, "O Lord, if I have found favor in your sight, do not pass by your servant" (Gen 18:3).

21. Ps 46:10a.

made great promises to you just as he made great promises to Abraham. You're going to be King of Israel soon. In fact, yours will be the very kingdom that God promised to Abraham—Israel will be the great nation. God will see to that just as he saw to it that Abraham and Sarah had a son. He always keeps his promises, and it isn't necessary for you, David, to assist him in keeping them. He does that sort of thing alone. Anything Abraham tried to do on his own to hurry things along didn't work out for him, and if you try the same, it isn't going to work out for you either.

Abraham had to wait it out for a quarter of a century. It could have been that long or longer for David to see things set straight with Nabal too. As it turned out, he had to wait only ten days (v.38), but David didn't know that at the time. That wasn't the issue anyway, nor is timing the issue for any believer. The point is that no matter whether the time be long or short, believers must wait on the Lord and refuse to take matters into their own hands. It may be excruciatingly hard to do, but that is the essence of faith.

WAITING ON GOD BRINGS
ETERNAL RIGHTEOUSNESS

The astounding fact is that by simply waiting expectantly in faith for God to keep his promises, we are made righteous in the sight of God.[22] The implications of Abigail's urging David to call off his men, to wait, to trust the Lord alone, are mind-boggling. "David," she is saying, "this is a great *opportunity*. You have a choice: you can trust yourself and become a mass murderer, a terrorist and a fool. Or you can just sit still, trust God to take care of Nabal and everything else, and obtain eternal righteousness."

Abigail was speaking from experience. She had put up with a fool for a husband probably for many years, but she was waiting it out. She did what Abraham did. She trusted God. Surely she wanted deliverance from the bondage of the wicked fool Nabal's grip on her life. But whether God would so deliver her or not, that wasn't the issue. Whatever God had in mind,

---

22. "No unbelief made [Abraham] waver concerning the promise of God, but he grew strong in his faith as he gave glory to God, fully convinced that God was able to do what he had promised. *That is why his faith was 'counted to him as righteousness.'* But the words 'it was counted to him' were not written for his sake alone, *but for ours also.* It will be counted to us who believe in him who raised from the dead Jesus our Lord, who was delivered up for our trespasses and raised for our justification" (Rom 4:20-25) (emphases added).

and whether it took a long time or short, she would wait. She wasn't asking David to do something she wasn't already doing herself.

QUESTIONS FOR THOUGHT

1. Abraham is scripture's prime example of one who waited. What caused him to wait for so long a time, when God's promises to him and Sarah went unfulfilled? Are you now waiting for God to keep promises he's made to you? Are you willing to keep waiting? If so, what motives you?

2. Abraham and Sarah had many doubts along the way. Did their doubts mean they had lost their faith in the Lord? Have you had, or do you now have, doubts? Have you lost your faith?

3. How did Abigail speak faith to David? In what ways would David's exercise of faith have helped him in the temptation he faced, that is, to kill Nabal? Did David's lack of faith that God would handle Nabal mean that David lost his faith in the Lord?

7. MY WAY

From infancy on, we want to do things on our own, and in our own way. That is so because by nature we want the credit. We want our name to be the one in lights, not someone else's—not even God's—if it means we won't be noticed. In the flesh, we have an insatiable craving for glory and acclaim.

OLD BLUE EYES

The late crooner Frank Sinatra put this human craving to music in his song "My Way."[1] In that hit, released in 1969, he claims that he got what he got out of life by doing things his own way. He claimed that the person that does so doesn't kneel to anyone, and intimates that he doesn't get anything of value if he does.

Perhaps the lyricist who wrote "My Way" was simply being honest about his life. If so, his life was a sad tale. The song is true for the person who does not have the Lord in his life. All he's got is himself because he has rejected God, and so must do things all alone. Such a life is terrifyingly lonely, hopeless and doomed to failure.

When I first heard Sinatra sing this song in 1975 on my car radio it made me shudder, and it still does. It's utterly godless and should make any Christian shudder. You're not going to speak the words of the one who kneels? If you are a Christian, you have knelt already, you continue to kneel, and you live by the testimony of the One who kneeled.[2] That's what the

1. Sinatra, "My Way."
2. "And [Jesus] withdrew from them about a stone's throw, and knelt down and

Christian life is all about, because only by kneeling before the Creator God can we enter the Kingdom of Heaven or live a life pleasing to him on earth. Nor is it a one-time event. Our entire lives must be lived in the kneeling posture. David, like every one of us, needed to bend the knee.

NOBODY WANTS TO KNEEL

Yet there is something deep within us—believer or unbeliever—that resists kneeling before anything or anyone. It was in David. It's the "my way" nature and it's ominous when it rears its head. As Christians we know that sin has no dominion over us—that is an absolute guarantee.[3] But in Romans 7 the Apostle Paul wrote that we are still subject to sin, because we are not yet made perfect.[4] Thus I should not be surprised when I am tempted to do things "my way." But when I yield to that temptation, I am singing right along with Sinatra.

Abigail anticipated "My Way" three millennia prior to its 1969 release. David, as evidenced by his urgent command to level Nabal's house with the sword, was going his own way. He wasn't going to kneel to anyone. He wasn't conscious of the fact that he was at a major crossroad in his life.

DAVID'S HEART DESIRE

But what did David really want, deep down in his heart? If he had thought about it even for a moment in the light of what God had already taught him, he would have called off the Nabal raid on his own, or never ordered it in the first place. But as noted in chapter 5, he was mad and when you're mad you've isolated yourself from the truth, from God, and from others. Abigail's mission was to pierce through that transient isolation.

David would become king of Israel, but he knew from the day Samuel anointed him on Jesse's farm that the kingdom would be something far

---

prayed" (Luke 22:41).

3. "For sin shall not have dominion over you: for ye are not under the law, but under grace" (Rom 6:14, KJV).

4. "So I find it to be a law that when I want to do right, evil lies close at hand. For I delight in the law of God, in my inner being, but I see in my members another law waging war against the law of my mind and making me captive to the law of sin that dwells in my members" (Rom 7:21-23).

greater than *his* kingdom. He knew and rested in the fact that it would be God's kingdom, and he would later glory in that truth:

> All your works shall give thanks to you, O LORD,
>   and all your saints shall bless you!
> They shall speak of the glory of your kingdom
>   and tell of your power,
> To make known to the children of men your
>   mighty deeds,
>   and the glorious splendor of your kingdom.
> *Your kingdom is an everlasting kingdom,*
>   *and your dominion endures throughout*
>   *all generations.*[5]

DAVID WAS NOT SENNACHERIB

Notice how vastly different this is from worldly kingdoms. The Davidic kingdom stands alone in history as God's kingdom. Pharoah's kingdom in Egypt was all about Pharoah, not God. Alexander the Great's Grecian kingdom was all about Alexander, not God. With the possible exception of the time when the emperor Constantine ruled, the great Roman empire was never about the living God. The Third Reich's unspeakably wicked kingdom was all about Adolph Hitler. The list of such kingdoms—some better but most worse—goes on *ad nauseum*. One of those we could name is Sennacherib, king of Assyria, an enemy of Israel during Hezekiah's reign. Sennacherib wrote this himself, hoping that it would convince historians of just how great a man he was:

> Sennacherib, the great king, the mighty king, king of the universe, king of Assyria, king of the four quarters (of the world); favorite of the great gods; the wise and crafty one; strong hero, first among all princes; the flame that consumes the insubmissive, who strikes the wicked with the thunderbolt. Assur, the great god, has [e]ntrusted to me an unrivaled kingship, and has made powerful my weapons above [all] those who dwell in palaces. From the upper sea of the setting sun to the lower sea of the rising sun, all princes of the four quarters [of the world] he has brought in submission to my feet.[6]

5. Ps 145:10-13 (emphasis added).

6. Luckenbill, *Ancient Records*, 115-16.

We don't know when King Sennacherib penned (or chiseled) this modest self-assessment, but it had to have been before he encountered Hezekiah on the outskirts of Jerusalem in 701 B.C. There, where Sennacherib's forces had surrounded the city, they besieged it to the extent that the Jews were starving to death, running out of water and about to give in to the Assyrians. But King Hezekiah prayed to Israel's living God, the one Sennacherib had just ridiculed:

> Incline your ear, O LORD, and hear; open your eyes, O LORD, and see; and hear all the words of Sennacherib, which he has sent to mock the living God.[7]

God answered Hezekiah's desperate plea and delivered Jerusalem by sending the angel of the Lord that very night, who quietly snuffed out the lives of 185,000 Assyrian soldiers encamped just north of Jerusalem: "And that night the angel of the LORD went out and struck down 185,000 in the camp of the Assyrians. And when people arose early in the morning, behold, these were all dead bodies!"[8] Sennacherib, tail between his legs, returned to his home base in Nineveh stripped of his army. He was then executed by his own two sons.[9] So much for "the flame that consumes the insubmissive."

That would not be David's kingdom, and yet, prior to Abigail's intervention he was planning to be a miniature Sennacherib himself. His ill-conceived plan to destroy Nabal and all his men was intended to advertise that *David* was the flame that consumes the "insubmissive." We should always be on our guard: the line between trusting in the living God and trusting in the arm of flesh is almost invisible. Abigail was sent to give David a divine reminder that this is not your kingdom to win "my way," but a kingdom to be bestowed upon you by the living God.

---

7. Isa 37:17.

8. 2 Kgs 19:35. The loss of Assyrian troops that night was nearly half the total deaths of American servicemen and women in World War II, in both the European and Pacific theaters of war, where the United States recorded 405,399 fatalities. United States: war fatalities1775-2023 | Statista, accessed 5/7/2023.

9. Isa 37:36-38.

ABIGAIL WAS INVASIVE

I believe that Abigail was treading carefully when she ventured into the next paragraph of her message:

> Please forgive the trespass of your servant. For the LORD will certainly make my lord a sure house, because my lord is fighting the battles of the LORD, and evil shall not be found in you so long as you live. (v.28)

She knew that she was invading an area that David may not consider hers to invade, so she begins with "Please forgive the trespass of your servant," meaning "if I'm overstepping my bounds here, I apologize beforehand." It would be hard for anyone to be offended after such a gracious, self-effacing preface.

But Abigail will be invasive. The right teaching and preaching of God's Word is always invasive. It is through the teaching of the Word that the Holy Spirit invades our "comfort zones"; that is, it can be excruciatingly *un*comfortable. In fact, if you have sat through, let's say, a year of preaching that has not made you uncomfortable at times you are probably not attending a church where there's biblical preaching.

I once knew a lawyer, older than me, who was by all accounts the best trial attorney in the state where I practiced. Occasionally we had opportunity to talk, and I would attempt to steer the subject toward the things of the Lord. He faithfully attended a local liberal Presbyterian church. We once talked about preaching, and he commented "I can't stand the kind of bible-thumping, fire-and-brimstone preaching that I've heard. When I attend church, I want to be comforted. Why would I even go to church if I can't find comfort there?" "Well," I responded, "I suppose some folks go to church because they hope to find the *truth* there." That ended our conversation.

Abigail proves to be invasive, and although graciously deferential to David, she will say what the Holy Spirit has commissioned her to say. She doesn't mince words but begins by telling General David that he's not the one in charge: "[f]or the LORD will certainly make my lord a sure house, because my lord is fighting the battles of the LORD" (v.28b) (emphasis added). She was stating for David's benefit a sure, divine promise. But in the context of David's plan regarding Nabal, it was also a rebuke, though a gentle and respectful one.

A SURE HOUSE

"My lord," Abigail was saying, "it is not up to you to build your house, but that's exactly what you are planning to do. If you follow through, you'll be attempting to bypass God, you'll be usurping his authority, and the house you'll be building will not be a sure thing. The house that God will build for you, on the other hand, will be a 'sure house.' Which do you want?" Abigail knew which one David wanted. She was reaching down into his heart. David wasn't a Sennacherib, a Pharoah or an Alexander. He wanted God's house and David's house to be one and the same. That is why he needed to appreciate the implications of what he was about to do.

God will build you a sure house, Abigail tells David, because "[you are] fighting the battles of the LORD." The nub of what she is saying is that "God will build you a sure house *so long as* you are fighting the battles of the LORD." She is also implying that his planned attack on Nabal would *not* be one of those "battles of the LORD." But she does state that David is a man who is fighting the battles of the Lord. She means that *that* is who the real David was.

FLY LIKE A JET

When my brothers and I reached our early teens and our parents considered us too old to spank after we had done something worthy thereof, Dad used to say the same kind of thing to us. He would take us aside after an offense and say "Boys, the Lord has made you to fly like jets. That's who you are as Christians. So fly way up there. Don't fool around with sin. You don't have to. Don't lower your landing gear. It'll get tangled with the treetops. You may well crash. Fly high; that's who you are." Dad was rebuking us by encouragement. Isn't it wonderful when someone scolds you in a positive way?

Job did the same. When Satan struck his home with disaster, killed all ten of his children, and inflicted him with life-threatening skin disease, his wife counseled him to "Curse God and die." Job answered, "You are talking like a foolish woman. Shall we accept good from God, and not trouble?"[10] Job was in fact attempting to encourage his wife, and saying something like this: "Honey, don't say things like that. Let's not give up on the Lord. You are talking *like* a foolish woman, but that's not the real you." Like Abigail with

---

10. Job 2:9-10.

David, Job was simply and kindly reminding his wife (and himself) of who they really were as a married couple ("shall *we* accept good from God, and not trouble?"), and the high calling they had as those who trusted together in the living God. It was rebuke by encouragement.

Abigail wanted David to remember who he was—a man who fights God's battles, not his own. She wanted David to fly way up there, not allowing his landing gear to tangle with the treetops by spending time and energy on his own ventures apart from the Lord. And she knew that that was what David really wanted too.

DAVID IS RIGHTEOUS BEFORE GOD

Abigail follows this with another assurance that may cause us to raise our eyebrows: ". . . and evil shall not be found in you so long as you live." Of all the promises that she recited for David, this one in particular stands out as one that Abigail could never have made on her own authority. The promise that another person could be one in whom "evil shall not be found" as long as he lives is one that only God could give. By its very nature, it could not be a human promise.

It might seem at first take that Abigail had departed substantially from what the Holy Spirit would have her say. God knew that David was headed for unspeakable sin in his life. In the Bathsheba scandal he would commit adultery, lie, steal and murder.[11] Later he would reject Joab's godly advice and take a census of Israel's fighting men, something Satan successfully enticed him to do in blatant disobedience to the Lord's command.[12] Those were two of David's more heinous sins, and David, like us, sinned in less spectacular ways every day of his life.[13] So what did Abigail mean by saying that evil would not be found in David as long as he lived?

David's meeting with the prophet Nathan is instructive here. One cannot imagine a more abominable and outrageous sin than David's

---

11. 2 Sam 11-12. The Lord himself later focused on David's sin with Bathsheba as being an exception in the life of a righteous man: "David did what was right in the eyes of the LORD and did not turn aside from anything that he commanded him all the days of his life, except in the matter of Uriah the Hittite" (1 Kgs 15:5).

12. 1 Chr 21:1-4.

13. "Surely there is not a righteous man on earth who does good and never sins" (Eccl 7:6).

stealing Bathsheba from Uriah, one of his mighty men,[14] and then having Uriah—a man who was fighting valiantly for David—courier his own death sentence to the frontline commander Joab.[15] When Nathan rebuked David, however, and announced some of some of the painful consequences of his sin, the Bible records this brief exchange:

> David said to Nathan, "I have sinned against the LORD." And Nathan said to David, "The LORD also has put away your sin; you shall not die."[16]

David's confession was immediate, but Nathan's assurance of canceled sin was even before immediate. Nathan could have said a number of things, like "I'll pray that God might forgive you, Your Highness," or "God is merciful, and he is able to forgive even this sin." Both responses would have been appropriate. But the Holy Spirit, through Nathan, assures David of something far more amazing: "The LORD also *has* put away your sin"! That divine act preceded David's confession. What the prophet Nathan was saying was what Isaiah later wrote:

> I will greatly rejoice in the LORD;
> my soul shall exult in my God,
> For he *has* clothed me with the garments of
> salvation;
> He *has* covered me with the robe of righteousness,
> as a bridegroom decks himself like a priest
> with a beautiful headdress,
> and as a bride adorns herself with her jewels.[17]

Abigail can assure David of something that applies to believers of all ages. Solely through the work of Christ, we are seen as righteous in God's sight. We do not need to wait for heaven to be adjudged righteous. The author of Hebrews said:

---

14. 2 Sam 23:39.

15. "In the morning David wrote a letter to Joab and sent it by the hand of Uriah. In the letter he wrote, 'Set Uriah in the forefront of the hardest fighting, and then draw back from him, that he may be struck down, and die.' And as Joab was besieging the city, he assigned Uriah to the place where he knew there were valiant men. And the men of the city came out and fought with Joab, and some of the servants of David among the people fell. Uriah the Hittite also died" (2 Sam 11:14–17).

16. 2 Sam 12:13.

17. Isa 61:10 (emphases added).

But when Christ had offered for all time a single sacrifice for sins, he sat down at the right hand of God, waiting from that time until his enemies should be made a footstool for his feet. For by a single offering he *has* perfected for all time those who are being sanctified.[18]

"He has clothed me with the garments of salvation" means that when God looks at the believer he sees his sinless son Jesus.[19] Paul said the same thing in Philippians 3.[20] Spotless. Perfect. Though she preceded the Lord Jesus and the Apostle Paul by a millennium, Abigail could assure David with divine authority that "evil shall not be found in you so long as you live." Though inconceivable to the natural mind, that is the essence of the Gospel, and Abigail was declaring it to her future husband and king.

GOD WOULD PROTECT DAVID

Abigail wasn't done with her message yet, though she could have stepped back from her donkey pulpit at this point because David was surely already convinced. But it was like church today. Just when you think the preacher is about to close it out, he rustles up another page of notes and continues. The congregants groan if the sermon has been dull up to that point, but Abigail's message had been anything but dull, and she could see that David wasn't groaning but actually taking notes. So she continued:

> If men rise up to pursue you and to seek your life, the life of my lord shall be bound in the bundle of the living in the care of the LORD your God. And the lives of your enemies he shall sling out as from the hollow of a sling. (v.29)[21]

18. Heb 10:12-14 (emphasis added).

19. "For we do not have a high priest who is unable to sympathize with our weaknesses, but one who in every respect has been tempted as we are, yet without sin" (Heb 4:15).

20. "Indeed, I count everything as loss because of the surpassing worth of knowing Christ Jesus my Lord. For his sake I have suffered the loss of all things and count them as rubbish, in order that I may gain Christ and be found in him, *not having a righteousness of my own* that comes from the law, but that which comes through faith in Christ, *the righteousness from God*" (Phil 3:8-9) (emphases added).

21. "For thus says the Lord: 'Behold, I am slinging out the inhabitants of the land at this time, and I will bring distress on them, that they may feel it'" (Jer 10:18).

LEAVE THINGS IN GOD'S HANDS

In the whole of Abigail's argument, but particularly from verse 28 on, the Lord is the protagonist, the moving force. He is the sole actor. David is not told expressly to take any action whatsoever. God will do it all. He will:

> make for David a sure house,
> protect David's life when he is pursued,
> bind David in the "bundle of the living" in God's
> care,
> sling out David's enemies as with a slingshot,
> appoint David as prince over Israel, and
> otherwise deal well with David all the days of his
> life.

Through Abigail, the Holy Spirit was telling David that his personal safety, victory over his enemies, gaining the throne, building his house and his life-long wellbeing were matters that he need not fret because God would handle every one of them for him, and far better than David could on his own.

PUSH THE PAUSE BUTTON

So David, don't take into your own hands those things that God has promised to do for you. Don't do things "my way." You don't need to go after Nabal. Call off your rangers, give them a day off tomorrow, and take them out for a company picnic. I've brought plenty of food—even some adult beverages. You "can eat your fill of all the food; you bring yourself!"[22]

There are times when we need to push the pause button on the remote. Slow down, relax, take a break and have a bite to eat. David should have done that because it would have given him time to think and pray. It would also have given him some rest.

God, for instance, has given us an entire day, once every week, to rest. It isn't meant to be an idle rest, but a time for worship and resting in God's promises.[23] It obviously runs contrary to the American way, which is a

22. Willson, *Music Man*, "You Ought to Give Iowa a Try."

23. *Westminster Confession & Catechism*, Shorter Catechism, Q 60, 420: "The sabbath is to be sanctified by a holy resting all that day, even from such worldly employments and recreations as are lawful on other days; and spending the whole time in the public and

twenty-four seven sweatshop. When we follow such a regimen, we work our-selves to death *and* lose our perspective as Christians. But like Abraham, we need to do more sitting at the doors of our tents in the heat of the day, simply basking in the great promises of God, waiting for God to do what he has told us he is going to do. Abigail tells David to take a break and do just that. God isn't asking you to do anything especially hard here, David, for his commands are not burdensome. His yoke is easy, and his burden is light.[24]

QUESTIONS FOR THOUGHT

1. Abigail was straightforward with David. Why did she feel the need to be invasive? Does it bother you when someone invades your "space"? Do you hesitate to do the same to others, even when you know you need to speak clearly to them?

2. Abigail encouraged David by assuring him that he was "fighting the battles of the LORD." When you have been on the cusp of sinning, has another Christian encouraged you in a like manner to "remember who you are"? Do you encourage others in a positive way, rather than merely rebuking them?

3. Why did David need to take a break, other than for physical rest? In the past, have you ever needed to take a spiritual break? What can be accomplished by doing so?

---

private exercises of God's worship, except so much as is to be taken up in the works of necessity and mercy."

24. 1 John 5:3; Matt 11:30.

8. BLESSED ARE THE PEACEMAKERS

A bigail's immediate mission in coming to David was to divert him from his plan to destroy her household. But the Holy Spirit would use her to do more than halt an attack. He would also use her as his means to help David gain—or regain—a right perspective on God's plan for him and for the great nation he would rule, God's chosen people Israel.

We are accustomed to hearing a benediction after a preacher finishes his sermon. A benediction is "the short blessing with which public worship is concluded."[1] Abigail, now at the end of the substance of her message, pronounces a benediction on her one-person "congregation":

> And when the LORD has done to my lord according to all the good that he has spoken concerning you and has appointed you prince over Israel, my lord shall have no cause of grief or pangs of conscience for having shed blood without cause or for my lord working salvation himself. (vv.30-31a)

This is a beautifully compact and perfectly composed sentence. Since Abigail didn't have time to put pen to paper before her meeting with David, it is evident once again that the Holy Spirit was working in her heart and mind as she spoke.

GOD'S BLESSING ON DAVID IS CERTAIN

Notice that Abigail's closing thoughts are all about David's future, and how the Nabal event bears on it. She first recites the fact that the Lord has

---

1. *Merriam-Webster,* "Benediction."

already secured that future; it's not up in the air or conditional. She says "*when* the LORD has done to my lord according to all the good that he has spoken concerning you . . ." Though she could have simply blessed David as in the sublime Aaronic benediction,

> The LORD bless you and keep you;
> the LORD make his face to shine upon you and
>   be gracious to you;
> the LORD lift up his countenance upon you
>   and give you peace,[2]

she went beyond that blessing. She was essentially telling David that "the Lord *will* bless you and keep you; the Lord *will* make his face to shine upon you; the Lord *will* give you peace"—he *will* do all these things because he keeps his promises. And he's made stupendous promises to you.

We can see again that Abigail wasn't assuring David of God's blessing based on her own authority; that wouldn't have been of any value. She was just a humble woman standing beside a humble donkey delivering a humble message from the Lord. As previously noted, in this way Abigail prefigured Jesus,[3] and David recognized the Voice that spoke through her. It was an assurance from God himself speaking by the Holy Spirit. David could, as they say, take it to the bank. He did take it to the bank, and he would draw on that bank account for the rest of his life.

CONSEQUENCES IF DAVID WERE TO IGNORE ABIGAIL'S MESSAGE

Though she does it in a subtly positive way, Abigail then gives David a glimpse of his future should he fail to heed her counsel. Think of when you become king, my lord. If you follow through with your plan tonight, you will always be dogged by the consequences. You're going to have a guilty conscience when you look back on this, and for good reason. You will have shed blood without cause, and you will have turned to your own way rather than the Lord's way.[4] You are going to be king regardless, but this day will be a dark memory; it will depress you; it will keep you awake

2. Num 6:24–26.

3. Zech 9:9; Mark 11:1–10.

4. "All we like sheep have gone astray; we have turned every one to his own way; and the LORD hath laid on him the iniquity of us all" (Isa 53:6, KJV).

at night; it will linger and haunt you; it will be a black mark that you absolutely don't want, or need, to have on your record.

GUILTY CONSCIENCE

A conscience, unless it has been cauterized by constant violation,[5] is a precious gift. It is fragile, too, and needs to be protected. One of the inestimable benefits of being a believer is that past sins are forgiven, and by the blood of Christ our consciences are cleared.[6] But how much better it is when we are able to turn from sin in the first instance, so that our consciences never have to deal with the matter. Abigail was endeavoring to keep David on track, so that he would never have to look back with regret on a bad day in Carmel.

WE NEED ABIGAILS IN OUR LIVES

In this regard, I have had many Abigails in my life, and wish I had had more. But there are innumerable times when I was on the cusp of making a wrong decision, one that would have led to sin, when someone came into my life to turn my head, to hold up a big Abigail stop sign. Usually, the person who was my Abigail wasn't even aware that they had turned my head from sin, but God knew, and I knew. I can look back at those times with no feelings of guilt at all, although when I think about just how close I came to taking a spill, I shudder, bow my head, and thank the Lord for his deliverance.

However, there are other times when no Abigail appeared, or if she did, I paid no attention to her. Sin was the result. I have asked for forgiveness and have solid assurance that God has forgiven me, and sees me as righteous in his sight. But I can also testify that I would have been far better off to have avoided the sin in the first place.

5. "Now the Spirit expressly says that in later times some will depart from the faith by devoting themselves to deceitful spirits and teachings of demons, through the insincerity of liars whose consciences are seared" (1 Tim 4:1-2).

6. "[H]ow much more will the blood of Christ, who through the eternal Spirit offered himself without blemish to God, purify our conscience from dead works to serve the living God!" (Heb 9:14).

PRECEDENT II

We have already seen in chapter 2 that David was concerned about precedent, as evidenced by his execution of the young man who claimed to have killed Saul on the battlefield. David didn't want it on the record that he had allowed someone to kill the Lord's anointed; that would be unacceptable precedent, particularly since he was headed for the throne himself.

Here, Abigail has just reassured David that God would put him on the throne, and she wants him to think about what kind of precedent he would set if he were to shed blood without cause. If it were a political campaign, David's slaughter of Nabal's household would become the opposing candidate's most touted theme. Think about your future, and the future of your country, my lord. Right now, your reputation is spotless. You can keep it that way. You don't want to set a precedent where a verbal insult like Nabal's would be legitimate cause for shedding blood—particularly not in Israel. Every Jewish citizen would feel freed up to follow your example. You would have blood in the streets. It would amount to legalized anarchy, the last thing you or any ruler wants for the country or for a legacy.

Abigail here was trying to protect the future King David and his kingdom from the present General David who, for a brief time, had become Hotheaded General David. She had gone well beyond merely seeking to protect her household from a raid. She is now seeking to protect the future kingdom from disorder.

PEACE

In all of this, Abigail was pleading with David for peace. Peace not just between David and Nabal, but between the present David and the later King David. Abigail wanted David to be at peace with *himself*. Peace not just for the next twenty-four hours, but for David's lifetime and for believers in the centuries to come. Peace not just externally, but peace in the heart. Hers was a full-orbed peace mission.

Calling off the attack David had planned for that night, apart from any other consideration, was of course critical. Had the attack materialized, there may never even have been a First Samuel Twenty-Five in the Bible. Although one never knows how a battle will end, Nabal and his men likely would have been slaughtered. David would have already shed innocent blood. But Abigail met her objective of preventing the shedding of innocent blood early on,[7] which would cause David and his troops to make a U-turn back toward their outpost in the wilderness. She had already brought about peace between warring parties. She could have gone back to Carmel waving a "mission accomplished" pennant. But she was treating for a greater, deeper, and more comprehensive peace.

ABIGAIL SPOKE THE "LORD OF PEACE"

When we read Abigail's argument to David, it is once again paramount that we recognize that more is going on than mere human speech. That is why David's first response to her speech was "Blessed be the LORD, the God of Israel, who sent you this day to meet me!" (v.32b). It was in fact a meeting between David and the Lord. It's too bad that this time David had not inquired of the Lord beforehand, but that didn't stop the Lord from showing up, even absent an invitation. He never needs one. We might say that God crashed David's party.

All that Abigail said to David was spoken as the Holy Spirit gave her utterance. There is no way that a 911 call from her servant just a few hours before she met David would have given her the requisite time as a mere human being to prepare anything on her own that would be worth our study, let alone inclusion in Holy Scripture. It was the Lord of peace[8] who spoke peace through Abigail.

It was a divine peace that the Holy Spirit brought to David's camp through Abigail. Everyone on site benefitted from her success in getting that night's raid canceled. It brought peace to Nabal, Nabal's servants, David, and David's 400 storm troopers. In particular, David's and Nabal's men had to have been greatly relieved that they didn't have to oppose each other in a bloody battle, because they had become compatriots out in the wilderness.[9]

There would be peace that night in Carmel, too, though the drunken Nabal[10] and his shearers were unaware of any threat to begin with. Carmel's

---

7. Recall that prior to any response from David, Abigail had said, "because the LORD *has* restrained you from bloodguilt . . ." (v.26b) (emphasis added).

8. "Now may the Lord of peace himself give you peace at all times in every way. The Lord be with you all" (2 Thess 3:16).

9. Nabal's servant, reporting to Abigail, had said of David's men, "They were a wall to us both by night and by day, all the while we were with them keeping the sheep" (v.16).

10. "And Nabal's heart was merry within him, for he was very drunk" (v.36b).

children could sleep soundly, undisturbed by the noise of clashing swords and the screams of dying men. But most importantly, Abigail had wrought peace between David and God, though in this respect David was a bit like Nabal and his shearers: he was unaware of any issue with God in the first place. (Had he inquired of God beforehand, he would have known that the Lord was not in favor of his plan.)

It has occurred to me, after studying Abigail's story, that in addition to her contemporaries on that day, she has brought peace to me, and I hope to you. We find tumult when we return insult for insult, try to do things our way, or try to build our own kingdoms. We find peace when we turn to the Lord before we strike out on our own, and listen to what he says through his word and our circumstances. We will find peace when we adhere to Abigai's advice.

PEACE TO THE PEACEMAKER

We must not overlook the fact that Abigail brought peace to herself as well as to others. After David had joyfully received her message, and accepted her gift, he told her to "[g]o up in peace to your house. See, I have obeyed your voice, and I have granted your petition" (v.35b). Peacemakers are beneficiaries of their own efforts. Whatever a woman sows, that shall she also reap. Paul states this both negatively and positively:

> Be not deceived; God is not mocked: for *whatsoever a man soweth, that shall he also reap.* For he that soweth to his flesh shall of the flesh reap corruption; but *he that soweth to the Spirit shall of the Spirit reap life everlasting.* And let us not be weary in well doing if we faint not.[11]

The principle here set forth, that people reap what they sow, is particularly applicable to peacemakers. He who sows the wind will reap the whirlwind.[12] But Abigail came to sow peace, and that is what she would reap. The Apostle James wrote:

> [T]he wisdom from above is first pure, then *peaceable*, gentle, open to reason, full of mercy and good fruits, impartial and

---

11. Gal 6:7–9, KJV (emphases added).
12. Hos 8:7a.

sincere. And a *harvest of righteousness* is sown in peace by those who make peace.[13]

A blessed canopy of peace descended that spring afternoon[14] over David's camp and the city of Carmel. Abigail had brought it, but it truly descended from above because it was the Holy Spirit who gave her the words to speak. It was a Holy Ghost peace. And her message of peace extended beyond the immediate. It extended far into the future—through David's reign, his entire life and beyond.

NO CAUSE OF GRIEF

Abigail told David that if he would countermand his own order to attack Nabal, then:

> . . . my lord shall have no *cause of grief* or *pangs of conscience* for having shed blood without cause or for my lord working salvation himself. (v.31a) (emphases added)

Surely there is not a person living who doesn't want what Abigail here promises David. Just close your eyes and think of a decision you made that was really, *really* bad. Have you not wished for an opportunity to go back in time to reverse your decision? Isn't the decision you made still a "cause of grief"? Although you've been forgiven by God—and hopefully by those you offended—it still brings grief. You wish for the opportunity to change that decision because of the pain it brought you, your family, and your friends.

I've had a problem with alcohol in my life, so it isn't hard for me to dredge up an illustration. If I have consumed that one-too-many martinis, the one that put me over the limit, then stagger into the car to pick up my granddaughter for her soccer game, cause an accident and injure the little girl as a result, I'll endure grief for the rest of my life. This is different from conscience, which will also bother me greatly, but the consequent grief will always be there in this life. Abigail says to all of us: if you reverse your present plan, for example, to drink that next glass of wine, you will avoid just a whole lot of grief in your life and in the lives of those who would have been hurt by your extra drink.

---

13. Jas 3:17–18 (emphases added).

14. Sheepshearing was, and still is, a springtime event in Israel.

ABIGAIL PURSUED INNER PEACE FOR DAVID

That is why we can say that Abigail's mission went beyond the immediate. She pursued an inner peace for David: absence of life-long grief and presence of a clear conscience. These things would be priceless for any person, but particularly for the king of Israel. And what was it that David would forfeit in order to obtain this peace? Just one absolutely worthless piece of trash: the brief moment of fleshly gratification he might get from killing a fool who had insulted him.

The word "peacemaker" typically is applied to someone who helps to reconcile two warring parties. Abigail was doing that: she brought peace between "David's side" and "Nabal's side." But she did it in large part by bringing inner peace to her lord David.

"Blessed are the peacemakers," Jesus told his disciples, "for they will be called children of God."[15] As a boy resembles his father, as a girl her mother, so peacemakers resemble their parent, the Prince of Peace.[16] Abigail was like her Heavenly Father when she spoke. Out there in the Wilderness of Paran, she brought the same message to the shepherd David that the angels brought to some other shepherds out there in a different wilderness near Bethlehem a millennium later on the first Christmas day: "Glory to God in the highest, and on earth *peace*, good will toward men."[17] This is not Abigail's, but God's peace, which he still speaks to the world.[18]

HOW BEAUTIFUL ARE HER FEET

In verse 3 of our text, the author tells us that Abigail was "beautiful." Perhaps the most beautiful thing about her were her feet, and I think Isaiah would agree:

> How beautiful upon the mountains
>   are the feet of [her] who brings good news,
> Who publishes peace,
>   who brings good news of happiness,

---

15. Matt 5:9, NIV.

16. Isa 9:6b.

17. Luke 2:14, KJV (emphasis added).

18. [T]he battle bow shall be cut off, and he shall speak peace to the nations; his rule shall be from sea to sea, and from the River to the ends of the earth" (Zech 9:10b).

Who publishes salvation,
who says to Zion, "Your God reigns."[19]

It is as though the prophet Isaiah was reading First Samuel 25 when he wrote Isaiah 52. For when she delivered her message to David, Abigail was in the mountains: "she rode on the donkey and came down under cover of the mountain, [and] behold, David and his men came down toward her, and she met them" (v.20). She brought good news: "the LORD has restrained you from bloodguilt and from saving with your own hand" (v.26b). We have already seen that this was a *fait accompli* even before she spoke, so it was truly *news*—God's restraining of David from these things had already happened—and very *good* news. In delivering this good news, Abigail also "publish[ed] peace" (considered earlier in this chapter) to David, his men, Nabal, his men, her household and even to herself. All of this was "good news of happiness," an echo in reverse from the message of the Christmas angel who announced a thousand years later "good news of great joy."[20] Or perhaps the Christmas angel was echoing Abigail. Either way, the two were resonating.

All the above is pretty convincing evidence that Isaiah had the truths in Abigail's message on his mind when writing his fifty-second chapter, but there is more compelling evidence to come, and it centers on the Author of our salvation.

QUESTIONS FOR THOUGHT

1. Abigail brought peace to David. To do a quick check on your memory, who else found peace because of Abigail? How was it that David obtained "inner peace" from what Abigail said? Have you ever helped to bring peace to warring parties, or to an individual who was at war with herself"?

2. This question is rhetorical: Are there any things you've done in your past that you regret? Do some of them still bring you "pangs of guilt"

---

19. Isa 52:7. *See also* Nah 1:15a: "Behold upon the mountains, the feet of him who brings good news, who publishes peace!" and Rom 10:15: "And how are they to preach unless they are sent? As it is written, 'How beautiful are the feet of those who preach the good news!'"

20. Luke 2:10.

from time to time? Would an Abigail in your life have helped? Are you invasive and loving enough to be an Abigail for others?

3. I once had an acquaintance, a Peruvian Christian, who told me he came to Christ because he was first attracted to the "beautiful feet" of the American missionaries that brought him to the Lord. What do you suppose he meant by that? Have you been attracted to such "beautiful feet"? Do you have a pair of them yourself?

9. SALVATION BELONGS TO THE LORD

W ho is this that comes from Edom,
    All his garment stained with blood;
To the slave proclaiming freedom,
    Bringing and bestowing good;
Glorious in the garb he wears,
    Glorious in the spoils he bears?[1]

Abigail answered Thomas Kelly's sublime question centuries before he propounded it. But before we look at her answer, consider Kelly's own, which is, in substance, Isaiah's:

'Tis the Saviour, now victorious,
    Trav'ling onward in his might;
'Tis the Saviour, O how glorious
    To his people is the sight!
Jesus now is strong to save,
    Mighty to redeem the slave.[2]

IT'S SIN EVEN TO TRY

Abigail reminded David by way of implication that he would be *sinning* if he attempted to save with his own hand.[3] It is sin for us even to attempt

1. Kelly, "Who is This?" stanza 1, from Isa 63:1: "Who is this who comes from Edom, in crimsoned garments from Bozrah, he who is splendid in his apparel, marching in the greatness of his strength? 'It is I, speaking in righteousness, mighty to save.'"

2. Kelly, "Who is This?"stanza 2.

3. ". . . because the LORD has restrained you from bloodguilt and from saving with

101

to do that which only God can do. As we have seen, it is sin to try to pry the keys out of God's hand. God actually searched for someone who could help, but

> He saw that there was no man,
>> and wondered that there was no one to
>>> intercede;[4]
> then his own arm brought him salvation,
>> and his righteousness upheld him.
> He put on righteousness as a breastplate,
>> and a helmet of salvation on his head;
> he put on garments of vengeance for clothing,
>> and wrapped himself in zeal as a cloak.[5]

We humans usually appreciate all the help we can get in our work, but it is not so with God in the matter of salvation. He not only doesn't need our help in saving us; he can't use it. Our attempts to save ourselves, or help the process along, are wrongheaded. We are prone to think that our good deeds will help us in our standing with God, but "[t]here is a way that seems right to a man, but its end is the way to death."[6] For us even to *offer* to help is blasphemy because salvation is holy ground—it is God's alone. We are simply not qualified to do what David was about to attempt, because

> [w]e are all as an unclean thing, and all our righteousnesses are as filthy rags; and we all do fade as a leaf; and our iniquities, like the wind, have taken us away.[7]

A FILTHY RAG MAKES THINGS WORSE

From my own experience, I know exactly what Isaiah is saying in this verse. Long ago, in those glorious sunshiny summer days of station wagons, excited children, family vacations and white sand beaches, we took a trip to the Atlantic coast in our Oldsmobile station wagon. But there is a downside

---

your own hand . . ." (v.26b).

4. Isaiah wrote: "But when I look, there is no one; among these there is no counselor who, when I ask, gives an answer" (Isa 41:28).

5. Isa 59:16–17.

6. Prov 14:12.

7. Isa 64:6, KJV.

to such happy vacations. We returned after two weeks of mosquitoes, butterflies and birds battling the Olds head-on. The birds and insects lost, their last memories being of our windshield. I had to clean it. I got out a bucket of warm water with some detergent mixed in, grabbed a rag from the garage, dipped it in the suds, and took a couple of big swipes on the glass. My intention, of course, was to make it spotless clean.

I should have looked more closely at the rag before using it. It was saturated with grime, grease, cigar ashes (she said that if there was any smoking of cigars it was for our garage only), and various other toxins and filth. Before the well-intentioned swipe of my rag, I could at least see well enough to drive, but now it was a big dirty smear, and a person couldn't see anything through it at all. It occurred to me on the spot that my filthy rag was exactly what Isaiah spoke of. It not only did the windshield no good but made it a whole lot worse.

That is why our "righteousnesses" (Isaiah puts it in the plural) are so odious to God. It is not that he is opposed to our visits to the widow or groceries for the orphan; indeed, those things are "true religion," and God requires them.[8] But when we fling those good deeds toward God in expectation that they will save us, impress him, or improve our standing with him, we miss the mark. We heave filthy rags and dirt and cigar ashes into the saving "fountain filled with blood, drawn from Immanuel's veins."[9] It is sacrilege, profanity, and blasphemy.

BESIDES ME THERE IS NO SAVIOR

The blood-spattered warrior that Thomas Kelly saw marching out of Edom was the Lord himself. "I, I am the Lord, and besides me there is no savior."[10] "And there is salvation in no one else, for there is no other name under heaven given among men by which we must be saved."[11] "Jesus said to him, 'I am the way, and the truth, and the life. No one comes to the Father except through me.'"[12] Abigail owned the same truth a millennium

---

8. "Religion that is pure and undefiled before God the Father is this: to visit orphans and widows in their affliction, and to keep oneself unstained from the world" (Jas 1:27).

9. Cowper, "There is a Fountain," stanza 1.

10. Isa 43:11.

11. Acts 4:12.

12. John 14:5.

before Jesus was born. She and David both knew that no human *can* "save with [his] own hand" (v.26b), or *should*. It is sin to try.[13]

Dispensationalism, in some forms, counters this truth. Cyrus I. Scofield, whose name is almost synonymous with dispensationalism, first published his widely read *Scofield Reference Bible* in 1909. It had significant influence in the 20th century, where many believing Christians read his interlinear commentary as though it were part of the text itself. Scofield did not intend for them to do so, but he did make some unfortunate statements in his commentary, perhaps the most famous of which was:

> As a dispensation, *grace begins with the death and resurrection of Christ* . . . The point of testing is *no longer legal obedience as the condition of salvation*, but acceptance or rejection of Christ.[14]

Scofield later qualified this statement, said the quote was isolated, and that critics had taken it out of context. But he did not delete it and much damage was done within the church for about a century just because his commentary was so widely used.[15]

Our consideration of dispensationalism here has much to do with Abigail's message. Dr. Scofield would have us believe that in the Old Testament, "legal obedience to the law" was "[t]he point of testing" for salvation. But Abigail, as directed by the Holy Spirit, would differ. She would equate Scofield's "legal obedience to the law" as the ground of salvation with "working salvation himself" (v.31b) and that is precisely what she told David was sin.[16] It is, in fact, the ultimate sin because it rejects Christ as our Savior. Abigail spoke bedrock Gospel; Scofield's statement spoke the opposite and is heresy. Abigail would probably not call Scofield a "heretic," nor would I. But she would rightly say that his statement amounts to the rankest of heresies because it strikes at the vitals of the Christian faith, that "*salvation belongs to the* LORD"[17] and to him alone.

13. Abigail positions "saving with your own hand" and "working salvation himself" in parallel with "bloodguilt," deeming them both to be sin from which David must turn (vv.26b, 31b).

14. Scofield, 1115 (emphases added).

15. Before the end of the twentieth century, however, Scofield's influence had waned substantially because of Christendom's increasing acceptance of reformed theology which rejects dispensationalism in almost all forms.

16. "For if it is the adherents of the law who are to be the heirs, faith is null and the promise is void. For the law brings wrath, but where there is no law there is no transgression" (Rom 4:14–15).

17. "Salvation belongs to the LORD; your blessing be on your people!" (Ps 3:8a), and

David knew from Israel's history that it was the Lord alone who had saved Israel—that salvation is wrought solely by him:

> [F]or not by their own sword did they win the land,
>> nor did their own arm save them,
> but your right hand and your arm,
>> and the light of your face,
>> for you delighted in them.[18]

BY GRACE ALONE

I have never met a person who has truly come to Christ who doesn't recognize that in the process it was God's grace alone that brought them, and they can sing for joy because they know that they couldn't have saved themselves. It has been done for us. Yet many who have known the Lord for many years are laboriously trying to please God by their works, apparently thinking that God's grace ceases at salvation but after that, it's largely up to us.[19] But if any of it at all were up to us, we are doomed to failure. The hymnwriter George Duffield wrote,

> The arm of flesh will fail you;
>> Ye dare not trust your own.[20]

David and Abigail understood well that the whole thing was by God's grace. They had "resonance"[21] in this, because when Abigail thanked the Lord for turning David from "working salvation himself" (v.31b), David immediately responded by thanking her and the Lord for stopping him from "working salvation with [his] own hand" (v.33b). They resonated not just between one another, but with true believers of all ages, before and after.

"I, I am the LORD, and besides me there is no savior" (Isa 43:11).

18. Ps 44:3.

19. The Westminster Assembly stated that our progression toward perfection (sanctification) is no more of works than is justification: "Sanctification is the work of *God's free grace*, whereby we are renewed in the whole man after the image of God, and are enabled more and more to die unto sin, and live unto righteousness." *Westminster Confession & Catechism*, Shorter Catechism, Q 35, 420 (emphasis added).

20. Duffield, "Stand Up for Jesus," stanza 3.

21. See discussion of "resonance" in chapter 5.

ANCIENT GRACE

We can go back as far as Abel, and even back to his parents. When Adam and Eve retreated into the thick of the orchard after eating the forbidden fruit, they displayed fear, weakness, and shame; they knew they couldn't face God in their present condition, so they tried to hide from him. They knew they couldn't extricate themselves from the catastrophe they had brought on:

> The moment that Adam ate of the fruit from the tree of knowledge of good and evil, sin was brought into the world,[22] "their eyes were opened, and they suddenly felt shame at their nakedness. So, they sewed fig leaves together to cover themselves."[23] Adam and Eve's attempt at making their own covering was man's first try to make himself right with God through his own efforts. But as the prophet Isaiah reminds us, our "righteous acts are like filthy rags"[24] [and] they can never wash us clean from our sin.[25]

Abel offered a blood sacrifice because the Lord had revealed to him that (a) he needed salvation, and (b) he could not bring it about on his own. His animal sacrifice was a foreshadowing of Someone who would do it for him. In our First Samuel text, David and Abigail testify to the same Gospel truth. And every believer between Abel and Abigail knew the same. Noah couldn't save himself and his family from the flood; God had to do it.[26] Abraham tried to manufacture God's promised heir on his own, but failed miserably; God had to do it.[27] Eliphaz, Bildad and Zophar, Job's three friends, tried to please God by their piety and preached to Job that he must do the same; that if—and only if—he did, his illness, pain and depression would vanish.[28] But the Lord deemed their efforts and advice as sin, and required Job to pray for them before they could obtain God's pardon.[29]

22. Rom 5:12 (Solberg reference).

23. Gen 3:7 (Solberg reference).

24. Isa 64:6 (Solberg reference).

25. Solberg, "Clothed in Righteousnes."

26. "[God] preserved Noah, a herald of righteousness, with seven others, when he brought a flood upon the world of the ungodly" (2 Pet 2:5b).

27. See subhead "Abraham Sat It Out" in chapter 6.

28. Eliphaz asked Job, rhetorically: "Is not your fear of God your confidence, and *the integrity of your ways your hope?*" (Job 4:6) (emphasis added).

29. God also required Job's three friends to make a burnt offering, foreshadowing Christ, the perfect sacrifice (Job 42:7–9).

These considerations demonstrate clearly that God's people in the Old Testament knew perfectly well that they came up hopelessly short when it came to "working salvation" (vv.31b, 33b) for themselves. They were not confused. We can go back to the phenomenon of resonance. Abigail merely mentioned "working salvation for himself" and David knew instantly what she was talking about. That is because, at bottom, all true believers from Abel to the present, understand that they cannot work salvation for themselves. But just as certainly, all believers, like David, need to be reminded of that truth along the way.

SWEET COMMUNION IN THE CHURCH

From Abel on, God has been building his church, the fellowship of believers. This holy fellowship resonates with what God has said in the Bible. It resonates with God himself. And as we come close to God, of course that brings us close to one another, and we find ourselves close to and agreeing with one another. David quickly agreed with Abigail because they both believed the Gospel; they had both come near to God. In the process, they had also come near to Abel, Noah, Abraham, Isaac, Jacob, Joseph, and every other believer in past ages, for the church is eternal—past, present, and forever:

> Yet she on earth hath union
>> with God the Three in One,
> And mystic sweet communion
>> with those whose rest is won.[30]

If Abigail had been sent to Abraham when he faltered (as he did), Abraham would have agreed with her too. If Abraham had popped up instead of Abigail to advise David, David and Abraham would immediately have found themselves of the same mind, and so on. At the very core of their agreement would be the most basic of gospel truths, which is that *salvation belongs to the* LORD.

QUESTIONS FOR THOUGHT

1. How does Thomas Kelly's hymn describing one who is coming out of Edom personify Christ? Why is he walking alone?

30. Stone, "The Church's One Foundation," stanza 4.

2. Why is it repulsive to God when we try to please him with our works, apart from his grace? What did Isaiah mean when he said that all our righteousnesses are like "filthy rags"?

3. What is the unifying source of our inclusion together in the church? Consider your relationships with other believers in the church. Do you find yourself in "sweet communion"? Do you have the same sense in your relationships with unbelievers?

10. ABIGAIL SPEAKS TO US

The message that Abigail brought to David is for us, Christians in the twenty-first century. Neither human nature nor the Gospel has changed. We are just like David—believing that God is sovereign, that he keeps his promises, that he will protect and care for us. But we are also like David in being prone, of a sudden, to take things into our own hands, inexplicably attempting to accomplish that which God alone can do.

STILL STRUGGLING WITH SIN

I say "inexplicably" and yet our taking things into our own hands *is* explainable to an extent, considering what the Apostle Paul said in the Book of Romans.[1] Though we are new creatures in Christ, the dying sin nature in us is still flailing away, wanting to take control. But it is a losing battle for the sin nature, so that Paul can exclaim, "Thanks be to God through Jesus Christ our Lord!" Romans 7 is truth for believers who are not yet made perfect,[2] which includes us all.

However, Romans 7 is only for believers, not unbelievers. Paul describes his struggles as between the new nature and the old; those who do not have faith in Christ cannot witness such a struggle precisely because they do not possess the new nature. The old nature stands unopposed in

1. "For I delight in the law of God, in my inner being, but I see in my members another law waging war against the law of my mind and making me captive to the law of sin that dwells in my members. Wretched man that I am! Who will deliver me from this body of death? Thanks be to God through Jesus Christ our Lord! So then, I myself serve the law of God with my mind, but with my flesh I serve the law of sin" (Rom 7:22-25).

2. Phil 3:12.

their hearts; the new nature has not yet intruded to give the old nature something to fight. Unbelievers may have struggles, but that described in Romans 7 is not one of them.

David, however, was a believer, and when Abigail met him he was struggling between the old nature and the new. The old nature urged him first to get very, very mad. He yielded. Then the old nature tempted him to take things into his own hands. He did. Then the old nature tempted him once again to make a plan to commit mass murder. He yielded yet again, and because he was so over-the-top angry, he commanded his troops to finish the bloody job before sunup the next day when, as the saying goes, "it would be all over but the shouting." So far (and that's pretty far) it doesn't look like there is any "new nature" in David at all. We are hoping that if it's there, it will raise its head before it's all over but the shouting!

David wasn't aware of these downward steps, nor are any of us when we are on a similar path. That's the problem. We are unaware of any danger, and someone needs to appear in our lives to open our eyes, to caution us as to where we are headed.

GOD'S TUNING FORK

But just in time—as is his habit—God sent Abigail riding on her donkey. By the unction of the Holy Spirit, she would awaken the new nature in her lord David—the dominant nature that had been in him all along—and trigger an about-face in David's life. As Paul said in Romans 7, "Thanks be to God through Jesus Christ our Lord!" David would soon join Paul in this short hymn of thanksgiving when he said to Abigail, after she had spoken, "Blessed be the LORD, the God of Israel, who sent you this day to meet me!" (v.32b).

Abigail could not have succeeded in her mission if her message had been to an unbeliever. There would have been no new nature to awaken. There would have been no resonance. What she said would have fallen on deaf ears—*dead* ears—ears such as her husband Nabal had. No one, her servant said, could talk to him (v.17). But Abigail could talk to David, because he had the Holy Spirit in him, who gave him ears to hear, ears that were open to what she had to say. Abigail would reverberate with David. She was God's tuning fork.

MR. MASON'S TUNING FORK

I've seen this kind of thing in real life. As a child, my seven siblings and I were required to take weekly piano lessons. Mom made us do that for a minimum of one year. After that, it was up to us. This was wise, because she knew that not all people were gifted the same, and that it wasn't necessary for everyone to play an instrument.

We used an old upright piano in our home to practice. Though some of its ivories had peeled off, it was a good piano, and remained so as long as it was kept in tune. My mother employed someone to do that, a Mr. Mason, and when he showed up, I made a point to watch him do his work. He used a tuning fork calibrated to "A" and would strike it to see if the pitch matched the "A" on our piano. In our case, it never did. Our piano always needed tuning.

When the Holy Spirit struck his tuning fork Abigail, it was to see if David was in tune. He wasn't. He was going his own way and was badly out of tune. Abigail was able to bring David back in tune, back into harmony with the Holy Spirit. Or, as Scripture says, she was enabled to help David "keep in step with the Spirit."[3] Paul beseeched the Christians in Galatia not to "gratify the desires of the flesh," but to "walk by the Spirit."[4] David, prior to Abigail's visit, was indeed trying to gratify the desires of the flesh. He was mad, he was venting, he was planning mass murder— just to gratify the fleshly desire to get back at Nabal for insulting him. From insult to murder, it was all a result of his not being in tune—that is, not keeping in step with the Spirit.

WE NEED TUNING

That is why we can say that Abigail speaks to all believers. We are like David because we have the propensity to gratify the flesh. We too can make a wrong turn; we can drift out of tune and need a Mr. Mason to cross the threshold with his tuning fork. But as believers, we have the Holy Spirit living within us. Like David, we will resonate with the truth if an Abigail rides

3. Gal 5:25, NIV.

4. "But I say, walk by the Spirit, and you will not gratify the desires of the flesh. For the desires of the flesh are against the Spirit, and the desires of the Spirit are against the flesh, for these are opposed to each other, to keep you from doing the things you want to do" (Gal 5:16-17).

up on her donkey and strikes her tuning fork. And if I sense no resonance with the Holy Spirit as she speaks, even though I think I am a believer, I must examine myself to see if I am being disobedient, or even to determine whether I truly am one of God's children.[5]

We can use what Abigail told David as a kind of "checklist" to see where we stand. He agreed with her immediately and wholeheartedly. She told David:

> that he was doing things his way instead of the
>   Lord's way,
> that he was therefore headed in the wrong direction, and
> that he was trying to bring about his own salvation.

The time for us to use this checklist is at the moment of temptation (of course that is exactly when we are most vulnerable, and most likely *not* to use it). However, it is also at such a time that the Holy Spirit awakens us and is most likely to intervene, and he will do the humanly impossible job of changing our heart, our affections, so that we actually *want* to use such a checklist. The Holy Spirit is not so much interested in our behavior; he is interested in the condition of our heart, and the great battles we face as believers are waged not on a visible battlefield, but in the unseen crevices of our hearts. That is where our affections reside.

GOD CHANGES OUR AFFECTIONS

This is one of the most astonishing things that God does this side of heaven. I know this to be true because I have tussled with my affections many times, and I simply cannot change them on my own. I can change my behavior for a time, but the battle goes on inside and if my affections haven't changed, nothing has been gained and the battle is ultimately lost.

As mentioned before, I have struggled with alcohol. In my desperation, I joined a "self-help" group where I met others struggling with alcohol, pornography, same-sex attraction and more. All of us were Christians, and all struggling mightily just to keep our heads above water. Perhaps we made some progress in that effort, but because the group was *self*-help, progress was short lived. I don't think a week went by when some member of the

5. "Examine yourselves, to see whether you are in the faith. Test yourselves. Or do you not realize this about yourselves, that Jesus Christ is in you?—unless indeed you fail to meet the test!" (2 Cor 13:5).

group hadn't reverted to his addiction, at least to a degree. The "self" can change only behavior, and that temporarily. It can never change affections. We, like David, need help from the Holy Spirit.

THE GOSPEL IS VERY GOOD NEWS

As Abigail told David: listen! (v.24b). The Gospel is very good news! We possess a new nature! God changes our affections by awakening in us our *dominant* nature. When we are struggling it seems anything but dominant, but that is where faith in God's word makes all the difference. The Bible tells us that the new nature is dominant whether we can see it or not:

> Therefore if any man be in Christ, he is a new creature: old things are passed away; behold, all things are become new.[6]

All the men in my self-help group believed the Bible, and we all believed this verse in our brains. Yet we were all sitting there in a circle, discussing our addictions that we knew we had no power to conquer by ourselves, feeling that it was utterly phony—even false—to say that "all things are become new." We were in that group just because all things were *not* new in our behavior, and we were trying to make that happen. We were attempting to make all things new on our own. But we couldn't.

MISSING THE MARK

Perhaps we were missing the mark. Our prayers were too often, "Lord, help me to stop dialing up porn on my laptop" when we should have been asking God to "awaken that incredible new nature that you have put in my heart so that I no longer have an *interest* in dialing up porn on my laptop." God can change behavior—he is the only one—but he's not interested in doing it just externally. God doesn't look at the things man looks at. He looks at the heart.[7] He wants to change us deep down inside and has promised that he will do so if we but ask. That is, if we ask in faith believing.

Our self-help groups were often gloomy events. We expressed hope but had little; seldom did I leave the meeting with a sense of victory. But I came to understand that at bottom, mine was an issue of faith: did I

6. 2 Cor 5:17, KJV.

7. "For the LORD sees not as man sees: man looks on the outward appearance, but the LORD looks on the heart" (1 Sam 16:7b).

believe God *would* change my heart if I asked him to, or did I merely believe that he *could* change my heart? And was I asking for something that God has already told me he would not give, that is, merely a change in my external behavior? God did not save us to be zombies, but brand-new people from the inside out. God wants us to change our behavior, but isn't impressed when we merely change our behavior. God will not mislead us by giving us a kind of half-baked success in changing our behavior alone. He will not allow us to become better behaved until we first ask him to change our hearts, our affections.

Consider the Pharisees. For more than a century before Christ appeared they had taught a theology of works, that is, of good behavior. If we look at the Lord's vehement denunciation of Phariseeism, we can see just how awful it would have been if Abigail had not come to meet up with David. Like the Pharisees, David was doing things his own way. Like them, he was trying to work his own salvation, just what the Pharisees taught.

This was David's sad state when Abigail showed up and reminded him of the truth: he not only should not, but *could* not work his own salvation. When Abigail got through to him, David was a very thankful man. He heaved a big sigh of relief. It had been a close call.

QUESTIONS FOR THOUGHT

1. David constantly struggled with temptation and resultant sin, as did the Apostle Paul. Were they abnormal? When you struggle with temptation and sin, are you able to remedy your propensities on your own? How did Abigail's message help David to go to the right place for help?

2. Using Abigail's message, examine your own walk with the Lord at the present time. She told David that he was doing things his way instead of the Lord's way, and was therefore headed in the wrong direction, trying to bring about his own salvation. What consequences awaited David if he had continued down such a path? How does doing things "my way" lead us to eventual disaster?

3. Why is it that changing bad behavior to good behavior without a heart change is ultimately impossible? Why is trying to change behavior alone odious to God? How is it that changing the affections of the heart will change behavior? What, or who, is necessary for working a heart change?

11. BUNDLE OF THE LIVING

A bigail recited many promises that God had made to David, among which were a "sure house," protection from his enemies, and ascent to the throne. But the most curious of her assurances was, "[i]f men rise up to pursue you and to seek your life, the life of my lord shall be bound in the *bundle of the living* in the care of the LORD your God" (v.29a) (emphasis added). What did she mean by "bundle of the living"?

BAGS AND BUNDLES

The Hebrew word for "bundle" can also mean "bag" or "pouch." For our purposes, the study of First Samuel 25, the translators evidently thought it would be better for David not to be stuffed in a bag or a pouch!—so they used the word "bundle."

The Hebrew word is used only ten times in the Old Testament. In Genesis 42:35 it refers to the Sons of Israel's pouches of money being carried from Egypt to Canaan. Job uses the word to describe God's grace in forgiving and forgetting our sins: ". . . you would not keep watch over my sin; my transgression would be *sealed up in a bag*, and you would cover over my iniquity."[1] In Proverbs 7:20 it's a "bag of money"; in Song of Solomon 1:13 it's "a bundle of myrrh." In Amos 9:9 it refers to a sieve that will not let precious stones fall to the ground. In Haggai the word is used negatively, speaking of God's judgment upon Israel for idolatry: "He who earns wages does so to put them into a bag with holes."[2] In the Book of Ruth it means

1. Job 14:16b-17 (emphasis added).
2. Hag 1:6b.

a "sheaf," one provided by Boaz as food for his poverty-stricken relative Naomi and her Moabite daughter-in-law, Ruth.[3] In each of these references, "bundle" or "bag" indicates that its contents are precious, significant, or important. It also implies that there is more than one thing inside (otherwise nothing would require "bundling" or "bagging"), and that the items inside are of the same kind, not a mixture of differing items.

ABIGAIL'S "BUNDLE"

Abigail assures David that he will be "bound" into such a bundle. David is precious; he is important and significant. The bundle contains other precious items too, essentially the same as David. This is not Haggai's bundle. This is a *good* bundle. It does not have holes through which David might drop out. It is safe and protective, and thus comforting. And, like most bundles, someone is carrying it, going somewhere, as in the Sons of Israel's money bags when they were headed back home to Canaan from Egypt.[4] It is a suitcase on the move, with a specific destination stamped on a tag tied to its strap.

LIVING STONES

However, this bundle is very different from other bundles because its contents are not coins or spice. Its contents are alive. If we look closely, we can see that things are moving about inside. Perhaps there are stones in the bag, but if so, they must be *alive*—they must be *living* stones.[5] Now we can identify them.

Abigail's "bundle" is a perfect metaphor for true Israel, that is, the Church.[6] Believers compose the Church, and they are the "living stones" that Peter spoke of. They are being bundled together. Abigail can assure

---

3. Ruth 2:16.

4. Gen 42:29-35.

5. "As you come to him, a living stone rejected by men but in the sight of God chosen and precious, you yourselves like living stones are being built up as a spiritual house, to be a holy priesthood, to offer spiritual sacrifices acceptable to God through Jesus Christ" (1 Pet 2:4-5).

6. Mathison, "The Church and Israel": "[I]f we are talking about true Israel, there really is no distinction [between Israel and the Church]. The true Israel of the Old Testament became the nucleus of the true church on the day of Pentecost."

David that if he is in danger from any foe, he will be safe because "the life of my lord shall be bound in the bundle of the living in the care of the LORD your God" (v.29b). So it is with every member of true Israel, the invisible church. Eschatologically, true Jerusalem is the Church, and it is being "built as a city that is bound firmly together,"[7] as in a bundle.

FLEEING AND BUNDLING

Abigail says that this "bundling" will happen to David when "men rise up to pursue [him] and to seek [his] life." At first glance, one might not think that "pursuit" has much to do with a bundle. But there is a direct relationship between the two.

"Pursuing" results in the pursued running away, fleeing from the one chasing him. We see this multiple times in the Bible as well as in our own lives. David was fleeing from Saul, who was pursuing him even as Abigail spoke. And think of Job. There, Satan was pursuing Job and Job was powerless to do anything about it. He "fled," not geographically, but in his spirit. What else could he do? God didn't seem to be intervening, despite Job's continual, desperate pleas for his help. Satan appeared to have the upper hand. In addition to the loss of all his property and death of his ten children, Job was left with a painful illness, such that he was sure he was going to die. It got so bad that Job *wanted* to die. Job wondered,

> Why is light given to him who is in misery, and life to the bitter in soul, who long for death, but it comes not, and dig for it more than for hidden treasures, who rejoice exceedingly, and are glad when they find the grave?[8]

Job was fleeing to escape his awful loss and pain, and lacking any other visible alternative, chose the grave as an attractive destination. But the Lord had a better port of call for him. He would have Job flee to him, and ultimately that is exactly where Job fled. Everything Satan did to Job drove him further and further into God's protective, loving hand—that is, into "the bundle of the living in the care of the LORD [his] God." Satan had not only wasted his time but got the exact opposite of what he had intended.

Abigail's bundle becomes a "safe haven" for believers when they are being pursued by foes. It is a "Mighty Fortress," as Martin Luther termed

---

7. Ps 122:3.

8. Job 3:20–22.

it, a haven for those who are fleeing from Satan, one far more powerful than they are, for "on earth is not his equal."[9] God's bundle is our only refuge. But there is no such bundle of refuge for those who do not have faith. They can find no safety from danger, no true or lasting comfort, for example, after the death of a child or some other horribly traumatic experience. God's bundle is made up of those of "like precious faith."[10] The author of Hebrews wrote:

> For good news came to us just as to them, but the message they heard did not benefit them, because they were not united by faith with those who listened.[11]

Those "united by faith" are bundled together in the Church because God enabled them to listen to the Gospel. Too often we fail to appreciate the tragic state of those who are not united by faith with those who "listened." Listening effectually to the Gospel simply isn't possible for us in the flesh. Yet Jesus gives the invitation to all: "He who has ears to hear, let him hear"[12]—and it is not an empty invitation, even though he has sovereignly chosen his own and bound them together in his care.[13]

STONES OF GOD'S CHOICE

We must also notice that believers are not the moving party in this "bundling." Stones, coins and myrrh do not collect themselves. God is the only one with the authority to determine who it is that will be bundled together with his church. He is the one who chooses them, just as one would choose which coins to put in his bag. And Abigail says that God is the one who would bind David into his bundle.

Jesus told his disciples about the difference between those who are gathered into his bundle and those who are not, those "fitted for destruction":[14]

> Another parable he put forth to them, saying: "The kingdom of heaven is like a man who sowed good seed in his field; but while

9. Luther, "A Mighty Fortress," stanza 1.

10. 2 Pet 1:1.

11. Heb 4:2.

12. Matt 11:15.

13. See chapter 5, ftn. 2, for Calvin's discussion of this mystery.

14. Rom 9:22, KJV.

men slept, his enemy came and sowed tares among the wheat and went his way. But when the grain had sprouted and produced a crop, then the tares also appeared. So the servants of the owner came and said to him, 'Sir, did you not sow good seed in your field? How then does it have tares?' He said to them, 'An enemy has done this.' The servants said to him, 'Do you want us then to go and gather them up?' But he said, 'No, lest while you gather up the tares you also uproot the wheat with them. Let both grow together until the harvest, and at the time of harvest I will say to the reapers, "First *gather together the tares and bind them in bundles* to burn them, but gather the wheat into my barn."[15]

The image in this passage is one of straw bundled together for the fire of judgment,[16] while the stalks of wheat are being gathered for bundling into sheaves, which will be threshed into something valuable, something a person can eat. The owner of the field will let both the weeds and grain grow together until time for harvest and then will make his choice known, a choice already made,[17] between the two. Wheat has nothing in common with straw. Jeremiah wrote:

Let the prophet who has a dream tell the dream, but let him who has my word speak my word faithfully. What has straw in common with wheat? declares the Lord.[18]

It is not given to us to understand or explain how that choice was made, but we join with Isaiah when he wrote,

O Lord, you are my God;
I will exalt you; I will praise your name,
for you have done wonderful things,
plans formed of old, faithful and sure.[19]

---

15. Matt 13:24–30, NIV (emphasis added).

16. Though a bundle of tares is worthless, and thus opposite to a bundle of wheat or coins, the parallel is striking. God holds two bundles, one composed of his saints and the other composed of the damned. The metaphor is intended to show the terrifying eternal separation one from the other.

17. "[God] chose us in him before the foundation of the world, that we should be holy and blameless before him. In love he predestined us for adoption to himself as sons through Jesus Christ, according to the purpose of his will" (Eph 1:4–5). *See also* chapter 5, ftn. 2, for John Calvin's discussion of the mystery of predestination.

18. Jer 23:28.

19. Isa 25:1.

ZECHARIAH'S STICKS

The prophet Zechariah graphically portrays this truth not in terms of coins, stones or grain, but sticks. His is a sort of YouTube video of Satan, the great accuser, standing next to Joshua the high priest, accusing him:

> Then he showed me Joshua the high priest standing before the angel of the LORD, and Satan standing at his right side to accuse him. The Lord said to Satan, "The LORD rebuke you, Satan! The LORD, who has chosen Jerusalem, rebuke you! Is not this man a burning stick snatched from the fire?"[20]

The image is one of the Lord rushing about, picking up sticks—even snatching some from the fire which is threatening to consume them if he doesn't hurry—gathering[21] and then tying them together to place into his bundle. The Lord also implies that Joshua will not be alone, but will be together with his "chosen Jerusalem," the Church—with David and every one of us who believes.[22]

A SIEVE

Amos has yet a different way of describing the same divine action. His is by way of a "sieve" (the same word as "bundle" in Hebrew). This sieve is a bag full of holes, but its holes are there for a good reason: to separate dust, dirt and debris from the stones, that is, to purify the sieve's contents: "For behold, I will command, and shake the house of Israel among all the nations as one shakes with a sieve, but no pebble shall fall to the earth."[23]

The shaking can be excruciating. We, the living stones, may be badly bruised as other stones hit us, but not one of God's precious stones—not even pebbles—shall fall out. They will remain safely in God's bundle. Jesus said that he will keep us there:

---

20. Zech 3:2, NIV.

21. "I will bring your offspring from the east, and from the west I will gather you" (Jer 43:5b). *See also* Jude 23, where Jude commands believers to do the same: "[S]ave others by snatching them out of the fire; to others show mercy with fear, hating even the garment stained by the flesh."

22. ". . . if, in fact the Spirit of God dwells in you. Anyone who does not have the Spirit of Christ does not belong to him" (Rom 8:9b).

23. Amos 9:9.

My sheep hear my voice, and I know them, and they follow me. I give them eternal life, and they will never perish, and *no one will snatch them out of my hand*. My Father, who has given them to me, is greater than all, and *no one is able to snatch them out of the Father's hand*. I and the Father are one."[24]

UNBOLTED BUT BUNDLED

When I practiced law, I represented an Illinois pastor and his wife whose teenage son was killed when a motorist crossed into his lane and struck his bicycle. There is no adequate way to describe the heartbreak and anguish that these parents suffered in the loss of their son, even though they knew he was with Jesus. Their grief seemed unbearable.

Some months after the accident the boy's mother told me, "I feel myself becoming 'unbolted' from the world." She said this through tears, but it proved to be the beginning of recovery for her. Her statement was a profound reminder to me that "this world is not my home"[25]—her true home was with Jesus and her son in heaven. She could look forward to that. She found herself increasingly "bolted" to heaven, and increasingly "unbolted" from the world. In other words, she was being unbundled from the world while being bundled into Abigail's bundle. My client could feel that happening to her, and while the process was unspeakably painful, she was finding true comfort in God's bundle.

What my client felt was what Christians experience at a moment of great loss or trauma. There is an increasing attraction to heaven, while the things of earth become "strangely dim."[26] Things of this world, including our lives and the lives of our children, are temporary and insecure. Throughout our lives, in various ways, God brings us through pain and sorrow to find comfort in his arms. And he also shows us that we cannot endure such experiences without help. True enough, we know we are eternally secure in Christ. We are in God's bundle, no one can take us out, and we are confident of our heavenly home. God has a firm grip on his bundle.

24. John 10:27-30 (emphases added).

25. Brumley, "This World," stanza 1.

26. Lemmel, "Turn your Eyes," chorus: "Turn your eyes upon Jesus / Look full in his wonderful face / And the things of earth will grow strangely dim / In the light of his glory and grace."

But there's that often painful "meanwhile." We have a difficult journey to take, one that we cannot endure alone. We need help every step of the way.

THE HOLY SPIRIT HELPS US
IN OUR PRESENT JOURNEY

David's "meanwhile" meant trying to stay alive. When Abigail came to see him he was fleeing Saul who had vowed to kill him. David would be safe one day in heaven, but the Saul threat was on today's calendar; it couldn't wait until heaven. Someone needed to help David on his journeys to the caves and to the wilderness and anywhere else he could hide. That was his current reality.

Abigail helped David, and she helps us, to gain confidence that we are being *presently* helped. She told David that "when men pursue you to take your life, you *are* in the care of the Lord your God" (v.29b) (emphasis added).[27] She wasn't talking here just of eternal security, or the safety of heaven. She was promising David that he would be safe from harm in the here and now. God would protect him in the present.

David couldn't make the journey apart from God's care. We can't either. And Jesus knew that we couldn't, and guaranteed us that help was on the way:

> And I will ask the Father, and he will give you another Helper, to be with you forever, even the Spirit of truth, whom the world cannot receive, because it neither sees him nor knows him. You know him, for he dwells with you and will be in you. I will not leave you as orphans; I will come to you.[28]

Why do we so often tremble with fear this side of heaven, considering such a rock-solid promise? Why do we doubt? We are not abandoned as orphans. We are not cut adrift. Jesus says here that God himself dwells with us and in us, and we should ask ourselves "what more can he say than to

---

27. The Hebrew word translated "care" comes from the root word meaning "with." Abigail's use of the word is consonant with Jeremiah's: "Fear not, *for I am with you*; I will bring your offspring from the east, and from the west I will gather you" (Jer 43:5) (emphasis added).

28. John 14:16-18.

you he has said, to you who for refuge to Jesus have fled?"[29] But he knows our weaknesses[30] and knows that we are ever in need of assurance.

ASSURANCE COMES THROUGH EARTHLY EXPERIENCES

David would learn through his earthly deliverances from Saul and other visible foes the eternal verity that God alone is the one who delivers. Again, he knew this to be a fact; the Lord had already delivered him from Saul's spear and sword.[31] But Abigail needed to remind David of God's promises for deliverance, because when she came to deliver her message, he was momentarily under the mistaken impression that David was the one who could deliver David.

It was through many troubles and trials that David increasingly realized that God was his deliverer. As we saw in chapter 1, he had learned as a child that God could deliver him from bears and lions. He was confident that God not only could, but would, deliver him from Goliath. God did, but he also kept after David to increase his confidence in him. He permitted Saul to place the death sentence on his head and chase him. David's entire life was besieged by threats and enemies. But Abigail's prophecy was fulfilled. Just as she said, God kept him safe in every case, "bound in the bundle of the living in the care of the LORD your God." David rejoiced in that eternal truth:

> He sent from on high, he took me;
> he drew me out of many waters.
> He rescued me from my strong enemy
> and from those who hated me,
> for they were too mighty for me.
> They confronted me in the day of my calamity,
> but the LORD was my support.

29. Rippon, "How Firm a Foundation," stanza 1.
30. "For we do not have a high priest who is unable to sympathize with our weaknesses, but one who in every respect has been tempted as we are, yet without sin" (Heb 4:15).
31. 1 Sam 19:10–12; 1 Sam 24:10.

He brought me out into a broad place;
he rescued me, because he delighted in me.[32]

CHRISTIANS NEED TO BE REMINDED THROUGH THEIR EARTHLY EXPERIENCES

We are in constant need of reminders that God is the one who delivers. Time and time again he has taught me this eternal truth through earthly means. He has delivered me from the spears and swords of my life, including financial distress, life-threatening illnesses, near-miss accidents, sin, middle of the night assaults by Satan, and many more personal threats. God has graciously delivered me from every one. What's more, like the Apostle Paul, I know that he will continue to try me and deliver me until the day I die. Paul said so when he wrote to the church at Corinth:

> We do not want you to be uninformed, brothers and sisters, about the troubles we experienced in the province of Asia. We were under great pressure, far beyond our ability to endure, so that we despaired of life itself. Indeed, we felt we had received the sentence of death. But this happened that we might not rely on ourselves but on God, who raises the dead. *He has delivered us from such a deadly peril, and he will deliver us again.* On him we have set our hope that he will continue to deliver us[.][33]

Paul, though an apostle, needed reminding. When he says that his troubles "happened that we might not rely on ourselves but on God," he means that even though he knew and preached that he needed to rely on God, he had to keep learning of his need to rely on him, and that his ongoing trials were constantly keeping him "up to date."

We should not get discouraged or down on ourselves if we must keep learning the same lesson over and over again. If David and Paul needed constant reminders to trust the Lord for deliverance, it's no wonder that we do. Trusting the Lord is not flat line. It is continuing, an upward curve. It was the *apostles* who asked Jesus to "increase our faith,"[34] thereby implying (a) that they already possessed faith but (b) that their faith needed to grow.

32. Ps 18:16–19.
33. 2 Cor 1:8–10, NIV (emphasis added).
34. Luke 17:5.

So it is with every believer. So it was with David, and the Holy Spirit used Abigail to augment David's faith.

John Newton said: "I am not what I ought to be, I am not what I want to be, I am not what I hope to be in another world; but still I am not what I once used to be, and by the grace of God I am what I am."[35] Newton is not advising complacency, but he is counseling us not to become discouraged if we are not yet what we "ought to be," because it is by God's grace that "I am what I am."

Christians are bundled together with others of "like precious faith,"[36] and all of us are growing. In that growing process, we depend on the Holy Spirit as he enables others to assist us, just as David depended on the Holy Spirit as he enabled Abigail to so assist him. What a marvelous bundle!

THE TIE THAT BINDS

My father, who I mentioned earlier as the pastor of a small church in rural Iowa in the 1950's, conducted Wednesday evening Bible study and prayer meetings in the homes of the farmers who were members of the church. This was done on a rotating basis, so we could enjoy the hospitality of one another in each home. Dad would always close the meetings by going around the circle of believers, shaking their hands and hugging them, while leading us in singing the first and last verses of John Fawcett's famous hymn, "Blest Be the Tie That Binds":

> Blest be the tie that binds
>> Our hearts in Christian love;
> The fellowship of kindred minds
>> Is like to that above.
> When we asunder part,
>> it gives us inward pain;
> but we shall still be joined in heart,
>> and hope to meet again.[37]

Even at age eight, I felt "bundled" when our tiny congregation sang this hymn—children want to be bundled—but I didn't appreciate the

35. "John Newton Quotes" www.goodreads.com/author/quotes/ 60149.John_Newton, accessed 5/4/2023.

36. 2 Pet 1:1.

37. Fawcett, "Blest Be the Tie," stanzas 1 and 4.

awesome significance of the words. But I do now, and weep just reading these two verses. It's not just because of nostalgia for the early 1950s, either. It is because as I've grown into my late seventies, I want, I *need*, to be bundled more than ever. Abigail assures me that I am.

QUESTIONS FOR THOUGHT

1. Apart from the opinions of the author, what do you think is meant by Abigail's term "bundle"? Do you think it is an appropriate metaphor for the Church? If so, how do stones, jewels, myrrh, and such fit the metaphor?

2. Have you had to "flee" to Christ in the past? Why was that necessary, and as you look back, why weren't you able to handle things on your own? In the fleeing process, did other Christians help you? Did you have a sense of togetherness?

3. Abigail says that those in her "bundle" are "in the care of the LORD your God." What is the scope of the term "in the care of"—that is, is it meant to comfort David when he is pursued by his earthly foes, or does it mean more? What is its scope for us today? How is this a consolation to you, and, in particular, to the Church?

12. A KINGDOM BESTOWED

T he courageous lady who rode up on a donkey into David's camp was about to deliver a message that was radical. It was not at all what the world would call "wisdom." But that is not surprising, because Abigail was speaking the wisdom of the Holy Spirit, and the world laughs at such "foolishness."[1] That is why the unbelieving world laughed at Jesus.[2] Like Abigail, he also came riding on a donkey to deliver his message. And like Abigail's, it was radical.

THE FOOLISHNESS OF PREACHING

The Apostle Paul preached the Gospel. Those who came to believe recognized it as divine wisdom, but unbelievers scorned his message. Paul wrote, "Where is the wise? where is the scribe? where is the disputer of this world? hath not God made foolish the wisdom of this world? For after that in the wisdom of God the world by wisdom knew not God, it pleased God by the foolishness of preaching to save them that believe."[3]

Abigail's message would have been scorned, for example, by Sennacherib, whom we discussed in chapter 8. Sennacherib did not possess the wisdom of the Holy Spirit, but of the world. Had Abigail delivered her message to him, it would have fallen on deaf ears, and Sennacherib would have scoffed at her and what she had to say.[4] When Abigail spoke to David,

1. 1 Cor 1:18.
2. Mark 5:40.
3. 1 Cor 1:20-21.
4. "To whom can I speak and give warning? Who will listen to me? Their ears are

however, she was speaking to one who knew the Lord, and for that reason she could "impart wisdom" to him:

> Yet among the mature we do impart wisdom, although it is not a wisdom of this age or of the rulers of this age, who are doomed to pass away. But we impart a secret and hidden wisdom of God.[5]

David's spiritually mature ears, supernaturally opened by the Holy Spirit, could hear Abigail's message, which held the "secret and hidden wisdom of God."

ABIGAIL'S WORLDVIEW vs. SENNACHERIB'S WORLDVIEW

Abigail's worldview was radical because it was theocentric. Sennacherib's wasn't radical at all, because it was perfectly consonant with the wisdom of this world. His was Frank Sinatra's "my way" view;[6] it was "Sennach-erib-centric." He was simply falling into line with what everybody else believed; it was conventional wisdom. And Sinatra was doing the same; that's probably why his song was well accepted and sold so many copies. His message resonates with those who are captured by the spirit of this age, the spirit that rejects God in favor of self.

The world can't figure Christians out. When I was in my second year of law practice, I was a member of a firm in the small city of Muscatine, Iowa, banked on the Mississippi. In such small communities, lovely as they are, there usually isn't much trial work and I wanted to specialize in that as opposed to a "desk" practice. I made inquiry into firms in larger cities in Iowa and received an offer from a good litigation firm in Cedar Rapids— just what I wanted. My wife and I prayed about it, believed the Lord was leading us in that direction, and I accepted the offer.

I announced our decision to my partners who were already aware of my desire to move and was surprised when one of them said: "I don't want you to leave the firm, but I think you are doing the right thing. I've learned

---

closed so they cannot hear. The word of the LORD is offensive to them; they find no plea-sure in it" (Jer 6:10, NIV). Contrast David: "Oh how I love your law! It is my meditation all the day. Your commandment makes me wiser than my enemies, for it is ever with me" (Ps 119:97-98).

5. 1 Cor 2:6-8a.
6. See chapter 7.

that in making decisions you should always look out for Number One." I was embarrassed, and felt that as a Christian, I was being unintentionally rebuked. I apparently had given the wrong impression, because I believed that in making such decisions I should *not* just be looking out for Number One, but primarily for the Lord's will in the matter.

Sennacherib's description of himself[7] is a declaration of a "Number One" worldview *par excellence*. It is all about Sennacherib, start to finish. But Sennacherib isn't the exception to the rule. All of us, before regeneration by the Holy Spirit, are the same. In the flesh, we all believe that it's not only permissible but right and proper for it to be all about us, and we shape our lives accordingly. It is only when we come to Christ that we learn differently, when we learn to say with the Apostle Paul, that it is ". . . not I, but Christ . . ."[8] That is the true believer's worldview.

However, as we discussed in chapter 7, when Abigail met David, he was leaning a bit in Sennacherib's direction. Among other things, Sennacherib claimed that he was "the flame that consumes the insubmissive." What was it that David was attempting to do other than to consume Nabal the "insubmissive"? Yes, there is a Flame that consumes the insubmissive,[9] but it isn't David, it isn't Sennacherib, it isn't even Satan, or any other earthly power.

ABIGAIL'S WORLDVIEW

As discussed in chapter 5, Abigail's mission to David was to deliver him from the Number One, the "My Way," or the "Sennacherib" syndrome. She accomplished that, and quickly, because in his heart David knew full well that it wasn't all about him. He resonated with Abigail's worldview.

But David would not have resonated with my senior partner's worldview any more than I did. If he had, he would not have been "a man after God's own heart."[10] He could not have been God's choice as King of Israel. He could not have been what the prophet told David that he and his offspring would become:

> The LORD declares to you that the LORD himself will establish a
> house for you: when your days are over and you rest with your

7. See p. 117ff.

8. Gal 2:20.

9. Nabal was "insubmissive," but the text informs us that after Abigail's meeting with David, "about ten days later the LORD struck Nabal, and he died" (v.38b).

10. 1 Sam 13:14.

ancestors, I will raise up your offspring to succeed you, your own flesh and blood, and I will establish his kingdom. *He is the one who will build a house for my Name, and I will establish the throne of his kingdom forever.*[11]

AN EVERLASTING KINGDOM

David's kingdom was to be an everlasting one. This is not a mere metaphor; it refers to a real, live, continuing "kingdom forever." It is the kingdom of the better and greater David, the Son of David.[12] It is impossible for us to fully comprehend, but that is the kingdom which Abigail, by the Holy Spirit, was undertaking to aim in the right direction. Her mission was proactive; David had not yet taken the throne. God used her to help David gain perspective for when he did ascend to the throne. He needed to know what his kingdom was, where it was coming from, and where it was going. Mostly, he needed to know who it was who would be building the kingdom.

In the above passage from Second Samuel 7, Nathan told David that "the LORD himself will establish a house for you." This is what Abigail said, almost verbatim: "For the LORD will certainly make my lord a sure house" (v.28b). David needed to remember that, because in his pursuit of Nabal he was attempting to build his house by himself and in his own way. That wouldn't do; it would not be a sure house; it would not be eternal. There is no record in the Bible of anyone having told that to David previously; perhaps Abigail was plowing fresh ground. But David surely knew that God would be the builder of his kingdom, and Abigail refreshed his memory, one that had hiccupped due to a flash of temper.

It is instructive for us to look at other scripture, for the Kingdom of Heaven is "bestowed" upon anyone and everyone who are true children of God. For example, each of the tribes of Israel, once they had taken possession of the Promised Land, received an "inheritance," that is, their share of the real estate.[13] Throughout the biblical record, the land of Israel is referred to as God's bequest to, or bestowal upon, the Jews. In the New

11. 2 Sam 7:11b-13, NIV (emphasis added).

12. "Behold, the days are coming, declares the LORD, when I will raise up for David a righteous Branch, and he shall reign as king and deal wisely, and shall execute justice and righteousness in the land" (Jer 23:5). The "Branch," of course, is Jesus.

13. Josh 13ff.

Testament, Paul refers to it as our inheritance in Christ;[14] Peter describes "an inheritance that can never perish, spoil or fade; [an] inheritance kept in heaven for you."[15]

IT'S ALL ABOUT GOD

In reviewing Abigail's speech, it is helpful to see what she said, and what she did not say. We have set this out previously, but here is what she said, in summary form:

> *God* will make for David a sure house,
> *God* will protect David's life when he is pursued,
> *God* will bind David in the "bundle of the living"
>   in God's care,
> *God* will appoint David as prince over Israel, and
> *God* will otherwise deal well with David all the
>   days of his life.

These five blessings are assured. Abigail then closes this section of her message out by adding, "And when the LORD has done to my lord according to all the good that he has spoken concerning you and has appointed you prince over Israel . . ." (v.30) (emphasis added). God, God, God, God, God, and the LORD! But Abigail, what about David? And what about all the rest of us, who want to be part of the action?

IT'S ALSO ABOUT US

Now as to what Abigail did not say. She did not tell David that he was to stand idly by, hands in his pockets, as he watched the Lord do all that he had promised. True enough, she did admonish him that he *should* "stand idly by" when it came to murdering Nabal!—but David still would have plenty of productive, adventurous, and even dangerous things to do. David would become the most mentioned person in the Old Testament, and other than Jesus, in the Bible as a whole.

It is not surprising that David is mentioned so often in scripture. God would call upon him to lead his band of six-hundred men, and later his

14. Eph 1:11.
15. 1 Pet 1:4.

great armies (including David's thirty-seven "mighty men")[16] who would gain victory after victory, until all the nations surrounding Israel had been subdued.[17] He would conquer Jerusalem, initiate it as the capitol city of Israel, populate it and bring the Ark of the Covenant there, thus establishing Jerusalem as the venue of worship for all Israel.[18] He fought many battles in his forty-year reign and never lost one. He would reign over all the tribes of Israel and from his throne would act as a royal judge.[19] He would compose songs and hymns for the people of Israel and become known as "the sweet psalmist of Israel."[20] He played the harp. He led the people of Israel in worship. His work was endless. When Abigail convinced David that he should refrain from killing Nabal, it meant that David could take a day off, but it likely would be his *last* day off.

THE KINGDOM IS GOD'S

Yet God would do it all. David, like you and me, was privileged to be a participant, but neither he nor any of us has the wisdom or the power to "save with our own hand" (v.26), make for ourselves a "sure house" (v.28), bind ourselves into the "bundle of the living" (v.29) or any of the other astounding things that God has promised to do for his saints, his church. That is why Jesus told the disciples that "*I will build my church.*"[21]

Lest we feel left out, consider where we would be if it were up to us to build the Kingdom. Could we guarantee a "sure house"? one that would last forever? Could we choose those who are placed in the "bundle of the living," bind them together, care for and preserve them eternally? Could we appoint the one to sit on the throne of the Kingdom of David, to rule forever? If we had to answer "no" to any of these questions, and if the church is to be built at all, we are all disqualified for the position of "builder." For one, I must admit that it's above my pay grade, so count me out. I wouldn't take the job even if offered. We are disqualified, but greatly relieved. When Jesus

---

16. 2 Sam 23:8-38 contains a full listing of these warriors, together with a summary of some of their heroic acts.

17. 2 Sam chapters 8-9.

18. 2 Sam 6:1-19.

19. "So David reigned over all Israel. And David administered justice and equity to all his people" (2 Sam 8:15).

20. 2 Sam 23:1b.

21. Matt 16:18 (emphasis added).

said, "I will build my church," we can say nothing but "Thank you, Lord!" and take great comfort in knowing that it is in his hand alone, and that it is *his* kingdom. God himself is the coin of his realm.

And what a glorious kingdom! It is glorious now and will be infinitely more glorious in heaven, where every living stone will be eternally bundled together "in the care of the LORD your God" (v.29). Bundled together now and bundled together then. From "glory to glory."[22]

THE KINGDOM IS OURS

This kingdom God has given to us, his Church. It belongs to us. We have inherited it. We possess it now and forever. It is not a kingdom that we have built or are building. It is a perfect kingdom because God alone is its builder. It is altogether a gift; it is a "kingdom bestowed" upon us.

That is why it is so important for us to grasp the whole of Abigail's message to David. He could not bring salvation by his own hand. He could not join himself into the "bundle of the living." David could not build a perfect, eternal kingdom. He could not on his own do anything that would help him at all to fulfill the great promises God had made to him. God knew, and Abigail knew, that if David was to gain *this* kind of kingdom it would have to be bequeathed to him. It could not be earned, because it would not then be a "sure house." If David were required, if we were required—or even allowed—to pay even as much as a penny for it, all of God's promises would vanish.[23] It must be bestowed upon us. And Jesus says it is:

> Fear not, little flock, for it is your Father's good pleasure to give
> you the kingdom.[24]

22. "But we all, with open face beholding as in a glass the glory of the Lord, are changed into the same image from glory to glory, even as by the Spirit of the Lord" (2 Cor 3:18). *See also* Eph 3:20–21: "Now to him who is able to do far more abundantly than all that we ask or think, according to the power at work within us, to him be *glory in the church* and in Christ Jesus throughout all generations, forever and ever. Amen" (emphasis added).

23. Naaman the Syrian learned this at his conversion when the prophet Elisha refused to take payment from him for his healing: "[Elisha] said, 'As the LORD lives, before whom I stand, I will receive none.' And [Naaman] urged him to take it, but he refused" (2 Kgs 5:16). *See also* Isa 55:1: "Come, everyone who thirsts, come to the waters; and he who has no money, come, buy and eat! Come, buy wine and milk without money and without price."

24. Luke 12:32.

QUESTIONS FOR THOUGHT

1. In what way was Abigail's message radical? Why would anyone think it to be so? How was it different from a message given from one who is not a believer? But also, why did David not consider her message to be radical, but quickly resonated with it?

2. Why do unbelievers scratch their heads when Christians tell them about how believers make decisions and live their lives? What are some fundamental differences between a Christian worldview and a secular worldview?

3. Why is it important for us to know that God's kingdom is his kingdom, one bequeathed to us? Why was it important for David to understand this, particularly at the time of his meeting with Abigail? What would it mean if we had earned the kingdom, or if we had been allowed to?

13. THE DEATH OF NABAL

There is more to the story. David's initial plan was to kill Nabal for scorning his request for food. Abigail had successfully turned David away from his plan to avenge himself, but God stepped in nevertheless and avenged David by taking Nabal's life. Nabal's untimely death happened like this:

After Abigail had finished her speech, her servants unloaded the donkeys and delivered the spread of food to David and his men. Having accomplished her mission, she bade David goodbye and returned to her home in Carmel. By this time night had fallen. It had been a busy day, and she surely wanted nothing more than to flop down on her bed. "But," she thought, "maybe first I should tell my husband what happened today. I suppose he has a right to know that his life has just been spared, how close he came to the end." It's possible too that she wanted to show the brute that she had done him a big favor, one that he didn't deserve. (Their marriage was on the rocks.)

So she went to her husband who was in the dining area, celebrating the valuable pallets of new wool with his cadre of sheep-shearers. She found her husband in the middle of serving up a great feast to the shearers, "like the feast of a king" (v.36). She also noticed that there were numerous drained wineskins and empty Johnny Walker Black bottles cluttering the floor and saw that Nabal was "very drunk"—in no shape to receive or understand any news at all, be it good or bad. She retired to her bedroom, deciding to wait until morning to give him the news. "So she told him nothing at all until the morning light" (v.36).

NABAL'S RUDE AWAKENING

The text that follows tells us what led to Nabal's death. "In the morning, when the wine had gone out of Nabal, his wife told him these things, and his heart died within him, and he became as a stone. And about ten days later the LORD struck Nabal, and he died" (vv.37-38). We are not told what exactly caused his death; to date, his death certificate has not been located by the archeologists. It is clear, though, that he was more than dumbfounded when Abigail "told him these things," but the extent to which she went into "these things" isn't mentioned.

It is very possible that she didn't tell him everything. Likely she didn't get the chance. Assuming she related the story to him chronologically, she would have started where *she* started, which was when the servant made the 911 call (vv.14-17). That, of course, was the news that David was planning to kill Nabal before sunup the next day. Nabal had a hangover, still reeling from his "very drunk" condition the night before. Maybe the news that David was planning to dispatch him before sunup was as far as Abigail could get before Nabal collapsed.

After all, it was morning by now, and it is likely that when Abigail told Nabal of David's plan to have him dead by sunup, Nabal frantically looked out the window, saw that the sun was *already* up, thought maybe that David and his band of men were running a bit late, and immediately went into shock from which he would not recover. Perhaps Nabal never got the news that Abigail had convinced David to call off the attack.

Abigail might have paused a bit after telling Nabal about David's original plan, just to see if it registered with the man about whom his servant had said, "he is such a worthless man that one cannot speak to him" (v.17b). Under normal circumstances, Nabal wouldn't listen to anybody. Well, this time he was listening—Abigail could see that he was *really* listening—but it was only for a second or two, because "his heart died within him, and he became as a stone" (v.37b). He was as good as dead. He was unresponsive, apparently never rousing from his coma. Ten days later, God "struck Nabal, and he died" (v.38b).

DAVID GETS THE NEWS

News of Nabal's death spread quickly, and when David heard about it, he didn't weep or even pretend to. Indeed, he was jubilant:

> When David heard that Nabal was dead, he said, "Blessed be the LORD who has avenged the insult I received at the hand of Nabal, and has kept back his servant from wrongdoing. The LORD has returned the evil of Nabal on his own head" (v.39a)

David's celebration of Nabal's death is in marked contrast to his reaction some years later when he was given the news of Saul's death. David was Saul's publicly declared enemy. He was number one on Saul's "most wanted" list. Saul had caused David a whole lot more trouble than Nabal had. Nabal wasn't pursuing David or seeking to kill him. All he had done was to send David an insulting memo. Saul had turned his pursuit of David into a royal career, but when David heard that Saul was dead, he "took hold of his clothes and tore them, and so did all the men who were with him. And they mourned and wept and fasted until evening for Saul and for Jonathan his son and for the people of the Lord and for the house of Israel, because they had fallen by the sword."[1]

It may seem odd for David to have mourned the death of someone who had murdered eighty-five of the Lord's anointed, innocent priests,[2] and had thrown a spear at him attempting to pin him up against the wall. When David eluded the spear, Saul sent his storm troopers out to kill him at his home.[3] Failing each of those attempts, Saul made it the centerpiece of his administration to kill David in the open field. Why mourn Saul's death, but not Nabal's? Nabal didn't make any attempts on David's life, nor, so far as we know, on anyone else's.

DAVID WAS THE GENUINE ARTICLE

If we look for an answer in merely human categories, we might think David was "faking it" when he wept for Saul. But David wasn't a fake. His character, as evidenced by his life, was one of transparency. When he was distraught, he couldn't hold it in. As his baby boy lay dying, David was overcome with anguish:

> David therefore sought God on behalf of the child. And David fasted and went in and lay all night on the ground. And the elders

1. 2 Sam 1:11-12.
2. 1 Sam 22:17-19.
3. 1 Sam 19:10-11.

of his house stood beside him, to raise him from the ground, but he would not, nor did he eat food with them.[4]

Nor could David hold it in when he was joyful, as when he "danced with all his might" when the Ark of the Covenant was brought up to Jerusalem:

> And David danced before the LORD with all his might. And David was wearing a linen ephod. So David and all the house of Israel brought up the ark of the LORD with shouting and with the sound of the horn.[5]

Audiences vary, as in this case; they can be all over the map. Michal, the daughter of Saul and David's wife, "looked out of the window and saw King David leaping and dancing before the LORD, and she despised him in her heart." But the female servants of Israel held David in honor.[6] David wasn't playing to the audience, so he wasn't much interested in whether they applauded or booed. He was just David being David, the man after God's own heart. God was his audience.

UNDERSTANDING DAVID'S MOTIVES

I think the key to understanding David resides in the foregoing two quotations, in the words "sought God" and "before the LORD." David's habit was to do everything he did "before the LORD." This is illustrated well in the chapter just before the story of Abigail, First Samuel 24. David was in the cave with his men when Saul unwittingly made himself vulnerable, and David's men wanted him to seize the opportunity to kill Saul. David refused:

> But David answered his men: "The LORD forbid that I should do this thing to my lord, the LORD's anointed, to put out my hand against him, seeing he is the LORD's anointed."[7]

Although scripture's record of David's life is replete with instances demonstrating his conviction that he had "only one person to please," I think this passage is perhaps the best. It is not merely an answer to his men; it is a record of David's thought processes, a tape recording of a man thinking

4. 2 Sam 12:16–17.

5. 2 Sam 6:14–15.

6. 2 Sam 6:20–23.

7. 1 Sam 24:6.

out loud. It is an example of when it is *right* to think things through. It is primarily David's answer to David, who was sorely tempted to follow his men's advice. Should he follow it, and get this Saul thing settled once and for all? That was a tempting prospect.

But David paused, giving himself time to think. We can hear him going over things in his brain. "No," he's thinking, "I know that the Lord would not approve; he would forbid it. If the Lord forbids it, so will I. And the reason that both God and I forbid it is that Saul is the Lord's anointed." Then, to bolster his developing conviction, he reminds himself a second time: ". . . seeing he is the LORD's anointed." The matter was settled. David had succeeded in putting himself and the Lord, so to speak, on the same page; he was keeping in step with the Spirit.

GIVE DAVID DUE CREDIT

This helps us as we attempt to decipher David's reaction to the news that God had taken Nabal's life. First, to say that he was happy only because Nabal was dead doesn't give David due credit. We have noted previously that in sin, David's first repair was to the Lord, that in blessing, David's first response was to the Lord. Now we may add another: when David hears that a brutish man had died, he first *blesses* the Lord!—

> When David heard that Nabal was dead, he said, "Blessed be the LORD who has avenged the insult I received at the hand of Nabal, and has kept back his servant from wrongdoing. The LORD has returned the evil of Nabal on his own head." (v.39a)

As we saw in David's thought process in the cave, here we see further evidence of his predilection for placing everything in the context of "the LORD." He first blessed the Lord because he "has avenged . . ." This is the primary reason that David was joyful when he heard of Nabal's death. It was because it bore out a truth that David already knew from reading his Bible, a truth that Abigail had urged him to remember. It certified the truth of God's Word:

> Vengeance is mine, and recompense, for the time when their foot shall slip; for the day of their calamity is at hand, and their doom comes swiftly.[8]

8. Deut 32:35. David's son Solomon would later write: "Do not say, 'I will repay evil'; wait for the LORD, and he will deliver you" (Prov 20:22).

It would be shallow exegesis if we saw David, after receiving the news about Nabal, kicking up his heels and doing high fives merely because an insult had been avenged. As if he were that childish or shallow. As if he were saying, "That's great, great, *great*! God has given me the one thing I've dreamed of, something I've always wanted out of life! The wicked witch is dead! Now I'll die a happy man. Bless the Lord, O my soul!"

No, it was more like "Amazing. *God* is amazing. He does avenge his children, just like Abigail, Moses and the Apostle Paul say. I don't need to take matters into my own hands, do things "my way," work my own salvation, build for myself a "sure house," or protect myself from those who are pursuing me to take my life. I can "[c]ast my burden on the LORD, and he will sustain me; he will never permit the righteous to be moved."[9] Once again, David knew all this long before he met Abigail, when she had to refresh his memory. But here it is as though the Lord is placing an exclamation point at the end of Abigail's message, as if to tell him: "David, what that woman told you ten days ago is *really true*!"

Believers often experience this in their lives. I know a Christian couple, a pastor and his wife, who had four children. They firmly believed God's promise that God would provide for his children; this pastor preached that truth regularly to his parishioners.

This couple were working as volunteers in an inner-city church. He was working on the side as a paper hanger to make ends meet, but suddenly the demand for his work stopped. There was an afternoon when they ran out of food, just enough left for a couple of days. They were desperate, and knelt down to pray.

As they got up from prayer, the telephone rang (the Lord doesn't always answer prayer so quickly!). A new customer needed a paper hanger immediately. Then the phone rang again: another customer. It kept ringing, and before nightfall he had more business than he could handle. God had provided, just as he said he would.[10] The couple was thrilled and amazed, just like David: "what that woman told you ten days ago is *really true*!" We know it beforehand, but when it actually happens, we are shocked.[11]

---

9. Ps 55:22 (altered).

10. Phil 4:19: "And my God will supply every need of yours according to his riches in glory in Christ Jesus."

11. An almost humorous example of such shock is recorded in Acts 12. Believers in Jerusalem stayed up late at night praying for Peter, whom Herod had imprisoned. When an angel delivered Peter from prison that night, a happy Peter came knocking on their door. A girl named Rhoda answered Peter's knock, and without opening the door rushed

God's protection of David would be a cause of joy for the rest of his life. He later wrote:

When they were few in number,
of little account, and sojourners in it,
wandering from nation to nation,
from one kingdom to another people,
He allowed no one to oppress them;
he rebuked kings on their account, saying,
"Touch not my anointed ones,
do my prophets no harm!"[12]

David is rejoicing because God, in striking down Nabal, is doing the same for David as he did for Abraham. Genesis 20 records the story of Abraham and Abimilech. Abraham's wife Sarah was endangered because of a lie that Abraham had told to Abimilech, telling him that Sarah was his sister, not his wife. But the Lord, instead of rebuking Abraham, punished Abimilech by "closing the wombs" of his wife and her maidservants. Although this seems upside down, it displays the extent to which the Lord will go to protect his "anointed."[13] God punished Abimilech for a seemingly trivial trespass—if any at all—on Abraham; likewise, God struck down Nabal for a seemingly trivial insult aimed at a believer.

It was crucial in this instance that God be the one who took Nabal's life instead of David. It was of paramount importance to David's coming kingdom, and thus the future king rejoiced at Nabal's death. David surely grasped that. If David had been the one who had taken Nabal's life, God would not have been in the equation. There would have been no cause for joy. But David can rejoice at Nabal's death because it is evidence of the extent to which God will protect his own—in this case, David, God's anointed one. Further, it was *immediate* fulfillment of Abigail's statement that ". . . when the LORD has done to my lord according to all the good that he has spoken concerning you . . ." (v.30a). And, we must remember, "The Lord is not slow to fulfill his promise."[14] Certainly such was true in this case.

---

to tell the praying believers that Peter had been freed. They told her she was out of her mind! (Acts 12:12-17).

12. Ps 105:12-15.

13. The Abimilech story is likely that to which David refers in Psalm 105. Abraham, in that story, was the "anointed." Abraham's troupe was "little in number," and Abraham was a sojourner, wandering from nation to nation.

14. 2 Pet 3:9a.

This is a comfort of comforts to Christians. God's promise to do everything necessary to protect Abraham and David from harm is not just for them. We are all God's anointed: "You have been anointed by the Holy One."[15] To our own detriment, we often forget what it means to be one of God's anointed. It means that we are *special*. We enjoy a wall of protection that is not available to unbelievers. As God's anointed, we have obtained that protection not because of what we do, but who we are. That is why God did what he did when Abraham lied to Abimilech. In spite of that lie, God favored Abraham with an impenetrable wall of protection. It didn't mean that God approved of the lie, but that God will protect his anointed simply because they are his anointed: his own name is at stake. It is altogether by "the grace in which we stand."[16] We have astonishing privileges that obtain only to those who are secure within God's bundle of the living. That is why David rejoiced, why Paul rejoiced in Romans 5:2, and why we can rejoice with them today. It is not so much a matter of "what we are" as "who we are." We are God's chosen people.

ABIGAIL MARRIES DAVID

Possibly the Bible's placement of an exclamation point after Abigail's name nudged David over the edge, causing him to do something he had not been free to do before Nabal's death. It is just possible that David's jubilation was in part due to the prospects suddenly opened for him. Abigail had ended her message with an invitation to David, not knowing at the time what was in store, when she said: "And when the LORD has dealt well with my lord, then remember your servant" (v.31b). Well, nobody needed to jog David's memory:

> Then David sent and spoke to Abigail, to take her as his wife. When the servants of David came to Abigail at Carmel, they said to her, "David has sent us to you to take you to him as his wife." And she rose and bowed with her face to the ground and said, "Behold, your handmaid is a servant to wash the feet of the servants of my lord." And Abigail hurried and rose and mounted a donkey, and

15. 1 John 2:20a.

16. "Therefore, since we have been justified by faith, we have peace with God through our Lord Jesus Christ. Through him *we have also obtained access by faith into this grace in which we stand, and we rejoice* in hope of the glory of God" (Rom 5:1-2) (emphasis added).

her five young women attended her. She followed the messengers of David and became his wife. (vv.39b–42)

We also noted the statement in scripture that Abigail was "discerning and beautiful." She had displayed both qualities to David when she first came to meet him. There's no debate about her beauty. But I think a legitimate question to raise is whether her assent to marry David was all that discerning.

MULTIPLE WIVES?

The creation story makes it clear that God intended marriage to be between one man and one woman: "Therefore a man shall leave his father and his mother and hold fast to his wife, and they shall become one flesh."[17] God designed us to be monogamous. He never expressed his approval of polygamy in the Old Testament (though it does appear that he tolerated it).

That's not so much the question. The question is, why did the women of the Old Testament tolerate it, God's standards aside? Polygamy has been practiced hardly at all since the close of the Old Testament era, and human nature hasn't changed. Polygamy is patently bad. What woman in her right mind wants to share the intimacy of marriage with another woman, or even women? For that matter, what man wants to have more than one wife, trying to assure both or all that they are the "love of his life"? David's son Solomon followed his father's example, only on steroids. As a result, he had to spend his life trying to convince each one of his 1,000 flames[18] that I Only Have Eyes for You.

NO FAIRY TALE

Second Samuel 25 is not a fairy tale, nor does it end like one. The author does not attempt to sanitize unwelcome, stubborn facts here, claiming that David and Abigail "lived happily after." Surely they had their good moments, for they had a son born to them, Chileab,[19] but multiple wives is a bad recipe for happy lives. Poor Chileab had to share his bedroom

17. Gen 2:24.

18. "[Solomon] had 700 wives, who were princesses, and 300 concubines" (1 Kgs 11:3).

19. 2 Sam 3:3.

with twenty or more brothers born to David and his eight wives (Abigail wasn't his last wife),[20] and we know almost nothing about how many daughters David had. We do know from scripture that David, not surprisingly, had to deal with unending conflict in an increasingly growing but dysfunctional family.

Maybe that is why the story of Abigail ends with the record of her marriage to David. It is a study in contrasts: the Abigail delivering a Holy Spirit message to David as compared to the Abigail agreeing to become one of David's multiple wives. Perhaps the Lord did not hold it as a sin against David or Abigail, but it was surely unwise. It does not appear that the Holy Spirit had directed Abigail in this, as he had in sending her to see David on her first trip. The second trip was to give him her hand in marriage. This was her decision, not the Lord's.

GOD'S UNCONDITIONAL GRACE

Abigail and David were mortals, subject to missteps. This is true for us too, and much too typical, even after we have heard the Word of God proclaimed. We often walk out after Sunday's sermon and blank out for the rest of the week. Abigail, by the Holy Spirit, had told David that the Lord would build for him a "sure house" and yet both she and David immediately took it upon themselves to build David's house, and humanly speaking, it turned out to be not so good a house. Abigail had told David that he should call off his plan to kill Nabal, which would have been doing things "my way," but she and David quickly departed from such a path by doing things "our way."

But, as Abigail had implied in her message, God will sweep our missteps, our weaknesses, our sins aside. He will do what he has promised to do *regardless*. As Abigail said, David *will* have a "sure house," he *will* be "bound in the bundle of the living" and his enemies God *will* "sling out." Nothing that David or Abigail might do, whether foolish or wise, could alter God's course. These are not "may it be so" statements but "it will be so."

God's promises are "regardless." It was by reminding David of this truth, and its eternal implications for him, that Abigail was able to turn David's head from evil to good, from depending on himself to casting himself

---

20. "David also took Ahinoam of Jezreel, and both of them became his wives. Saul had given Michal his daughter, David's wife, to Palti the son of Laish, who was of Gallim" (1 Sam 25:43–44).

upon the Lord, and from disaster to blessing. In the end, that is exactly what David wanted, and what he needed.

QUESTIONS FOR THOUGHT

1. David was jubilant when he heard that Nabal had died. Should he have been? Why or why not? What difference do you see from the way he reacted to the news of Nabal's death as compared with Saul's death?

2. What can we learn about David from the fact that he "sought God" and did what he did "before the LORD"? What does it mean for us today? Can you say that you seek God in your decisions, and that you do what you do *before the Lord*?

3. When you have strayed in your life (assuming that you have!) have you had to come to a new understanding of God's unconditional grace?

14. REMEMBER YOUR SERVANT

I n her speech to David, Abigail urged him to do many things to change his course of action. But her urgings were largely by way of implication—strong implication, to be sure—but she made no outright demands. Nor had she made any request for herself, for Nabal, or for her household. She rightly honored David as royalty, as a prince that would soon be king; that is why she continually addressed him as "my lord." This was wise, and her implications were not lost on her audience.

ABIGAIL'S REQUEST

Abigail ends her speech, however, with a personal request that she could not afford to leave to mere implication, lest there be any gaps in communication, or misunderstanding:

> And when the LORD has dealt well with my lord, then remember your servant. (v.31b)

What was she asking of David? Was it motivated by something like "You're going to be rich and famous someday, and then you'll probably forget all about me"? That doesn't fit the rest of her speech.

Abigail, in her final utterance, was asking for something much more than that David would just recall her. She had just painted a glorious picture for David of his reign over Israel. David's reign was certain; he would be protected from those who pursued him; he would be seen as righteous in God's sight; he would be bound into the bundle of the living; his enemies would be defeated and thrown out as from a sling—and in the process God, not David, would be building for him a sure house. All this was guaranteed. God would do nothing but bless David; he would bestow this glorious kingdom upon him.

In her plea, Abigail is saying this: "I want to be part of that kingdom. I too want to be protected from those who want to hurt me, to be seen as righteous in God's sight, to be bound into God's bundle, to have a sure house. I want to join you in your kingdom. Please remember me."

Abigail surely didn't know in specific what that might mean. She didn't know what David could even do to grant her request. All she knew was that she wanted him to remember her in a substantial way, a way that would substantially benefit her. That would have to suffice for now. The details could be spelled out later when David came into his kingdom, but she needed assurance that she would not be forgotten.

DAVID'S MEMORY

Abigail may not have realized it, but she was speaking to someone who had a very good memory. Saul's son Jonathan, who loved David like a brother, and who protected him when Saul was making repeated attempts on his life, made a request of David as well:

> "[D]o not cut off your steadfast love from my house forever, when the LORD cuts off every one of the enemies of David from the face of the earth." And Jonathan made a covenant with the house of David, saying, "May the LORD take vengeance on David's enemies." And Jonathan made David swear again by his love for him, for he loved him as he loved his own soul.[1]

Jonathan and his father Saul both died in a battle against the Philistines.[2] David became king, and when he took the throne, he searched diligently for someone in Saul's house to whom he could show favor, to fulfill his promise to Jonathan. David inquired of Ziba, a former servant of Saul: "Is there not still someone of the house of Saul, that I may show the kindness of God to him?"[3] Jonathan's crippled son Mephibosheth was located and brought to him. David awarded him Saul's entire estate and invited him

---

1. 1 Sam 20:15-17.

2. 1 Sam 31:1-6.

3. 2 Sam 9:3b. It is noteworthy that David does not say "my kindness" but "the kindness of God."

to eat at the king's table for the rest of his life. David didn't merely recall, he *remembered*, and there is a big difference.[4]

Perhaps one of the reasons that David remembered others was that as a child he had been forgotten. There was that bleak day on Jesse's farm, when his father and older brothers forgot him while they feasted with Samuel. It is heartbreaking to be forgotten. No, David wouldn't forget his oath and he wouldn't forget his friend Jonathan. He remembered. His memory was proactive, too: he didn't wait for Mephibosheth to come knocking on his door. He came knocking on Mephibosheth's door.[5] David's memory was intentional, sharply focused and determined. Samuel sought him out that day on Jesse's farm, and he would do the same for Saul's son Mephibosheth.

Abigail wasn't asking David to keep some memento of her stuck away in a photo album. She wanted real, live, substantial remembering—the kind of remembering that would have invited David to the feast with his brothers, the kind of remembering that did invite Mephibosheth to dine at the king's table for the rest of his life. Not mere recollection, but inclusion.

When we read Abigail's request, it's hard not to think of Joseph in Egypt. Joseph had been imprisoned by his master Potiphar, who, on the false testimony of his master's wife, had jailed Joseph on the charge of attempted rape. Joseph was rotting in jail when he interpreted the cupbearer's dream, telling him that he would be set free in three days and restored to his former office. But Joseph made a request of him: "Only remember me, when it is well with you, and please do me the kindness to mention me to Pharaoh, and so get me out of this house."[6] Once again, Joseph wasn't asking the cupbearer to just recall him; he wanted to be remembered in such a way that he could escape the dungeon.

The most poignant and oft recited word "remember" is in the celebration of the Lord's supper: "Do this in *remembrance* of me"[7] (emphasis added). Again, this is not speaking of mere recall or recollection. We remember

---

4. When a person signs his or her "Last Will and Testament," they typically leave something to their children, and often others. This is known as "remembering" or "including" someone in a testamentary document, not "recalling."

5. David here prefigured Christ in two ways: (a) in keeping the covenant he had made with Jonathan, thus blessing Jonathan's offspring, as God had done in honoring the Abrahamic covenant, thus blessing Israel, and (b) in diligently seeking that which was "lost" (Luke 19:10).

6. Gen 40:14. The cupbearer, however, forgot Joseph, remembering him a full two years later when Pharoah had dreams and needed an interpreter. (Gen 41:1).

7. Luke 22:19; 1 Cor 11:24.

Christ in his life, his death, and his resurrection. This is a life-changing remembering. It is transformational, an ongoing remembrance—not static, but dynamic. Remembrance of Jesus in all that he was is the difference between eternal life and eternal damnation.

GOD'S MEMORY

The Bible tells us much about God's remembering. It is never mere recall. The first explicit text is regarding Noah. He and his family were literally adrift in their lives, floating rudderless in a wooden box on top of unending oceans. It had been 150 days since the great flood began, and there was no land in sight. "But God remembered Noah and all the beasts and all the livestock that were with him in the ark. And God made a wind blow over the earth, and the waters subsided."[8] God's remembering was not just recalling—it was rescuing eight otherwise doomed souls. Now, millennia later, God is still remembering Noah. Four times every year we witness it. After the flood, God promised Noah: "While the earth remains, seedtime and harvest, cold and heat, summer and winter, day and night, shall not cease."[9] God has kept this promise four times every year and will continue doing so as long as the earth remains. God will never forget Noah or the promises he made to him. Through Isaiah, God states that the "remembering" he exercised with Noah is the same he exercises with all his children:

> "This is like the days of Noah to me:
>> as I swore that the waters of Noah
>> should no more go over the earth,
>> so I have sworn that I will not be angry with you,
>> and I will not rebuke you.
>> For the mountains may depart
>> and the hills be removed,
>> but my steadfast love shall not depart from you,
>> and my covenant of peace shall not be removed,"
>> says the LORD who has compassion on you.[10]

God also made stunning promises to Abraham, at least one of which was fulfilled in his lifetime, when Isaac was born. But many of God's

8. Gen 8:1.

9. Gen 8:22.

10. Isa 54:9-10.

promises were to be fulfilled much later. God has a very long memory. He had promised Abraham that from him would come a great nation— even "many nations,"[11] and during the next four hundred years Abraham's offspring had grown in number to more than two million. But they were being brutalized as slaves in Egypt,

> and the people of Israel groaned because of their slavery and cried out for help. Their cry for rescue from slavery came up to God. And God heard their groaning, and *God remembered his covenant with Abraham, with Isaac, and with Jacob.* God saw the people of Israel—and God *knew*.[12]

God "remembered" and "knew." This was more than mere recall and acquaintance. It meant deliverance from slavery for more than two million people. It meant that "the LORD [would bring Israel] out of Egypt with a mighty hand and an outstretched arm, with great deeds of terror, with signs and wonders."[13]

It is that kind of "remembering" that Abigail was requesting. She wanted and needed something powerful and effectual, a "remembering" that would seek her and find her,[14] a remembering that was proactive, personal, precise, and had muscle. Again, she didn't know specifically what David's kingdom would look like, but she knew that she wanted to be included. She also knew that it would be a "sure house," for she said that in her message, but she didn't know what the Lord later told David, that his house would be both sure and eternal:

> And your house and your kingdom shall be made sure forever before me. Your throne shall be established forever.[15]

Thus, the eternality of David's house is incorporated into the term "sure house," whether or no Abigail apprehended the significance of the term. While David's earthly line appeared to have ended with King Zedekiah in 587 B.C. when Babylon sacked Jerusalem, it was not in fact the end of the

11. Gen 17:5.

12. Ex 2:23b–25 (emphases added).

13. Deut 26:8.

14. "I will seek the lost, and I will bring back the strayed" (Ez 34:16a); "For the Son of Man came to seek and to save the lost" (Luke 19:10).

15. 2 Sam 7:16. *See also* David's last words in 2 Sam 23:5: "For does not my house stand so with God? For he has made with me an everlasting covenant, ordered in all things and secure. For will he not cause to prosper all my help and my desire?"

Davidic royal line. King Jesus was yet to come, also of David's line, and this Son of David "shall reign forever and ever."[16]

David could not build such a kingdom. God would be its builder. David could not earn it. God would give it to him. If mere man were to build or earn it, it would not be the Kingdom of Heaven. It would be earthly, temporary and faulty. It would end in abysmal failure, just as it ended when Nebuchadnezzar destroyed Jerusalem in 587 B.C. When shaken, it would fall. But the kingdom that God gave to David and to us is permanent and forever, so "let us be grateful for *receiving* a kingdom that cannot be shaken."[17] David's eternal kingdom was a *gift*; it was *bestowed* upon him.

Abigail asked David for inclusion in his kingdom, and both David and God heard her request. David answered for both: "Go up in peace to your house. See, I have obeyed your voice, and I have granted your petition" (v.35b). It was, and is, as simple as that for any man, woman or child who asks in faith, because "everyone who calls on the name of the Lord will be saved."[18] And how shall we escape if we ignore so great a salvation?[19]

As he was dying, the thief on the cross asked the same of the Son of David, who was hanging on a cross next to him: "Jesus, remember me when you come into your kingdom." Jesus responded to the thief as David did to Abigail: "Truly, I say to you, today you will be with me in paradise."[20]

"See," Jesus was saying, "I have granted your petition. Go up in peace to your house."

QUESTIONS FOR THOUGHT

1. What might have been on Abigail's mind when she asked David to "remember" her when he came into his kingdom? What does it mean to be "remembered" in a will? Have you ever felt that God has forgotten you? Where can you go for assurance that he hasn't?

2. Think of times in your life when you have felt excluded, when you wanted to be included. How did you feel? What did you do about it?

16. Rev 11:15b.
17. Heb 12:28a (emphasis added).
18. Rom 10:13.
19. Heb 2:3a.
20. Luke 23:42b-43.

3. Why is it important for us to understand that the Church is a divine institution? Can you give reasons for why the Kingdom of Heaven cannot be earned, and why it must be bestowed upon us?

15. ACKNOWLEDGEMENT

And David said to Abigail, "Blessed be the LORD, the God of Israel, who sent you this day to meet me!" And we say to Abigail, "Blessed be the LORD, the God of Israel, who sent you this day to meet *us*!"

BIBLIOGRAPHY

Black's Law Dictionary, Eleventh Edition, Thompson-Reuters, Minneapolis-St. Paul, 2019.

Brumley, Albert E., arr., "This World is Not My Home," author unknown, 1919.

Bulwer-Lytton, Sir Edward, the First Earl of Lytton (1831-91), A-Z Quotes | Quotes for All Occasions (azquotes.com).

Calvin, John, *Institutes of the Christian Religion*, edited by John T. McNeill, John Knox, 1960.

Cowper, William, "God Moves in a Mysterious Way," 1774.

———, "There Is a Fountain Filled With Blood," 1774.

Duffield, George (1818-1888), "Stand Up For Jesus."

Fawcett, John, "Blest Be the Tie That Binds," 1782.

Kelly, Thomas, "Who is This That Comes From Edom?," 1809.

Lemmel, Helen Howarth "Turn Your Eyes Upon Jesus," 1919.

Luckenbill, Daniel David, *Ancient Records of Assyria and Babylonia Volume 2: Historical Records of Assyria From Sargon to the End*, University of Chicago Press, OCLC 926853184, 1927.

Luther, Martin, "A Mighty Fortress is Our God," 1529.

Mathison, Keith, "The Church and Israel in the New Testament," Ligonier Ministries, https://www.ligonier.org/learn/articles/the-church-and-israel-in-the-new-testament, accessed 3/1/2022.

Merriam-Webster.com, https://www.merriam-webster.com, 8 May 2011, accessed 5/9/2023.

Rayburn, Robert S, *The Truth in Both Extremes: Paradox in Biblical Revelation*, Wipf & Stock, 2022.

Rippon, John, publisher, "How Firm a Foundation," in *A Selection of Hymns from the Best Authors, Intended to be an Appendix to Dr. Watts' Psalms and Hymns*, known as "Rippon's Selection," hymn 128, 1787.

Scofield, Cyrus I., editor, *Scofield Reference Bible*, New York: Oxford University Press, 1945.

Sinatra, Frank, "My Way," © Warner Chappell Music France, Jeune Musique Editions, BMG Rights Management, CONSALAD CO., Ltd, Suisa, Concord Music Publishing LLC.

Solberg, Stephanie, "Clothed in Righteousness: The First Sacrifice," *Making Him Known*, https://makinghimknown.tv/clothed-in-right-eousness-the-first-sacrifice/, 2/15/2020, accessed 2/6/2022.

Spurgeon, Charles Haddon, "Overcome Evil with Good," in *The Metropolitan Tabernacle Pulpit 22*, Passmore & Alabaster; James Paul; George John Stevenson; George Gallie, 1855.

Stone, Samuel John, "The Church's One Foundation," c. 1860.

Stott, John R.W., *The Cross of Christ*, InterVarsity, Kindle Edition, 2021.

Westminster Confession of Faith, together with The Larger Catechism and The Shorter Catechism, Revised Edition, John Knox, 1964.

Willson, Meredith, *The Music Man*, (1957–1961), Internet Broadway Database, accessed May 9, 2023.

SCRIPTURE INDEX

First Peter

Second Peter

First John

Jude

Revelation